Discovering Kenarchy

Discovering Kenarchy

Contemporary Resources
for the Politics of Love

EDITED BY

ROGER HAYDON MITCHELL

AND

JULIE TOMLIN ARRAM

WIPF & STOCK · Eugene, Oregon

DISCOVERING KENARCHY
Contemporary Resources for the Politics of Love

Wipf and Stock
An Imprint of Wipf and Stock Publishers
199 W. 8th Ave., Suite 3
Eugene, OR 97401

www.wipfandstock.com

ISBN 13: 978-1-4982-0060-8

Manufactured in the U.S.A.   09/09/2014

Contents

List of Contributors

Roger Haydon Mitchell is an honorary research fellow and partnerships coordinator for the Richardson Institute for Peace Studies in the Politics, Philosophy, and Religion (PPR) Department at Lancaster University. He has been working as a consultant to the church internationally for forty years and currently co-directs 2MT, a charity offering help and advice on negotiating change www.2mt.org.uk. He is married to Sue and has two sons and daughters-in-law and four grandchildren.

Julie Tomlin Arram is a journalist and co-founder of Digital Women UK, a project which aims to facilitate female creative practitioners to fully engage with social media. Her work, which focuses on women's activism, has been published by *The Guardian*, the *New Statesman* and *Huffington Post*. Last year she visited Athens twice to find out more about the impact of the economic crisis in the country and potential new initiatives.

Sue Mitchell is a former teacher who has pioneered women's leadership in often patriarchal church structures. She now functions in educational consultancy in support of school refusers and pupils educated other than at school. She is an accredited life coach practicing mainly in the areas of psycho-spiritual health and wellbeing. She is currently studying for an MSc in positive psychology and is a smitten grandmother of four.

Peter McKinney works in the community and voluntary sector in Northern Ireland, currently in the area of improving social inclusion and the life chances of young children, having spent the previous ten years delivering and developing support services to those experiencing homelessness, addiction, and marginalization in Ireland, North and South. He has an academic background in Literature and History and is keenly interested in how history and identity creation interact in social change.

Stephen Rusk is a doctoral researcher at Queen's University, Belfast. His main interests are in the ethical and political issues involved in gift, international relations, Europe, and the production of subjectivity. He has over twelve years' experience of promoting and advising others on social and organizational change.

Andy Knox is a husband to Kat and a dad to three beautiful children. He is a general medical practitioner in North Lancashire, the clinical lead for maternity services for North Lancashire and South Cumbria, a community partner of the Richardson Institute for Peace Studies, an academic advisor for the University of Manchester Medical School, and a keen blogger at www.reimaginingthefuture.org.

Mike Love works with Leeds-based charity Together for Peace www.t4p.org.uk, which he co-founded in 2003 after earlier careers in social housing, as a solicitor, and a church leader. Since its inception T4P has brought together many and diverse groups and people in Leeds and beyond to develop and support cooperative projects that strengthen communities and promote peace-making.

Martin Scott, an author of five books, hosts a blog that seeks to explore perspectives on the interaction of faith and post-Christendom Western society. His research degree, in the Eschatology of the New Church Movement, was a major impetus to explore an eschatology that is consistent with the incarnation.

Foreword

Julie Tomlin Arram

To BEGIN, WE MUST acknowledge that this book represents the work of two women and six men, all of whom are white. This regrettable lack of diversity is in tension with the book's key focus which is, as Roger Haydon Mitchell writes in the Introduction, to "give meaning" to the politics of love.

By focusing on the core that is at the heart of Jesus' politics—instating women, prioritizing children, advocating for the poor, welcoming the stranger, caring for the creation, freeing prisoners, and caring for the sick—the following chapters serve as both markers for our current position and an exploration of where kenarchy might lead us.

Each chapter represents an exploration within a particular field of a journey that "begins with and continues to multiply loving connections by emptying out whatever power one has in the direction set by the original encounter and then extended in ongoing relationship."

The question each of the authors raises, is the challenge of emptying out and subverting current power structures and how key questions facing us today can be reconceptualized in order that the interests of those at the margins are served, and not the interests of the few.

While not seeking to justify or explain away the Eurocentric imbalance in this book, we offer it as a starting point and motivation for discussion that we regard as being urgent, that is, what is required of us if we are to demonstrate a faith that is inspired by a self-emptying God?

The following chapters set out ways in which the hallmarks of kenarchy have informed the contributors' journeys. They tell of the questions raised by pursuing a relational approach to life, the collaboration and interaction with those marginalized by the sovereign exercise of power. The stories from chapter 2 onwards are contributed by people engaged in fields related to the specific foci prioritized by Jesus' own kenotic politics.

The first chapter is an attempt to plumb the depths of the love for one's enemies that the cross spans in order to further uncover this profound resource. It looks at the way in which the Jesus story re-patterns humanity through a transcending will to identify, to love, and to embrace, since the cross as the culmination of the life story is "the place where the non-violent God embodied in a non-violent humanity willingly takes the worst violence . . . and [deposits it] in the depth of their own being."

In chapter 2 I outline a comprehensive overview of sovereign power in its patriarchal guise and elision of women in the public sphere. Exploring the portrayal of woman as "other" and woman as victim and marginalized, I also raise the specter of the hegemonic culturalizing of feminism as an adapted sovereign project and advocate a kenarchic response to the power play by "white woman."

Referring again to our common human experience of being both victim and perpetrator of the sovereignty system, in chapter 3 Sue Mitchell "reads" some of the stories of a new vision of womanhood that began to emerge during the Puritan era and extrapolates their meaning for today's context.

In the fourth chapter, McKinney considers the criminal justice system and its binary analyses of these conflictual social roles, revealing its particular brutality again in relation to women and children. He calls for a restorative relational investment that breaks this "retributive cyclical dysfunction."

Rusk, in chapter 5, provides a theoretical basis for such a relational investment in considering gift in counterpoint to "the power of ownership to gain even more." He makes a compelling argument for a politics of love or gift and further exploration of its implications for macro-economics and geopolitics.

In chapter 6, Knox faces up to the particular issue of bio-power in healthcare. He suggests practical, individual acts of love to reconfigure power and challenge injustice daily but does not shy away from systemic commodification and issues of politicization that must also be tackled. He explores the possibility for a kenarchic leadership style which facilitates cooperative interconnectedness and participatory communities that include the voice of the otherwise marginalized in place of competitive interest groups.

In chapter 7, Love tells the story of struggling towards such participatory communities. Drawing tellingly on theories of peace-builders and academics he offers a reflective analysis of the bruising effects of intimidation and powerlessness, negotiating the challenges personally and organizationally. In the context of Leeds as a workshop for peace, they "learned ways to bring people together where all voices are listened to and shared wisdom discovered, where purpose is the invisible leader and leadership itself is redefined."

In the final chapter, Scott then recovers the radical hope of an eschatological vision with its counterpolitical purpose. He considers the colonizing effects of ignoring the ironic character of eschatology's imperial language and introduces a kenarchic hermeneutic that reinterprets its motivation and methodology to provide a future horizon for today's praxis such as outlined in the previous chapters. It is a vision that connects Jesus' incarnation story, via the tension and struggle of contemporary incarnational experiences, to a future hope for a new inclusive humanity where the margins have become the center and the call is for us to live authentically in the "space between the now and then" in the relentless pursuit of a new creation.

Introduction

Resources of Love
for Politics of Peace

Roger Haydon Mitchell

THIS BOOK, LIKE THE earlier companion volume *The Fall of the Church*, is for those motivated by the desire for a truly positive politics of peace. A kind of politics that can provide an effective, counterpolitical way of being in the inherently violent, socially divided, and decomposing society of our contemporary Western democracies and their burgeoning neo-capitalist counterparts like China, India, and Brazil. It is an attempt to supply resources for human flourishing that can lastingly empower non-violent action among and on behalf of the world's poor and oppressed wherever they are to be found. This is a way of life in pursuit of which a surprising diversity of people find themselves looking to the testimony of Jesus. The authors are well aware that the institutional religion in which the Jesus story has so often been submerged is regarded by many as the cause and character of the failure of the so-called Christian West. This secularist challenge might have made us nervous at the idea of embarking on a project that drew on the politics of Jesus. However, as the previous book, *The Fall of the Church*, has made clear, the contortions of both secularists and Christians stem from a mistaken common insistence on sovereign power as the means to peace. Our response has been to take courage from the current habit of agnostics and neo-Marxists alike, together with radical disciples of Jesus, and to make a draw on the love at the heart of Jesus' message as a means to configure a contemporary politics of peace. As the extraordinary Hannah Arendt has put it, "The discoverer of the role of forgiveness in human affairs was Jesus of Nazareth."[1] In focusing on Jesus the contributors are deliberately including those of other faiths or none. We deeply desire that many who regard Jesus as a great prophet, an idealized myth, one of many incarnations, or just a wonderful human being will come with us on our journey of discovery. We share this planet and are in need of a politics of love. It is with all this in mind that the initial chapter of the book unapologetically hones in on the core issues of incarnation and sacrifice basic to the politics of love for one's enemy that occupies the heart of kenarchy.

It was sometime in late 2009 that a period of creative discussion around a desire to cut through the negative baggage surrounding the implications of the phrase "kingdom of God" issued in the invention of the new word *kenarchy*. In March 2010 I wrote on my blog: "After the helpful and even fun discussions on the terminology of the kingdom of God I am seriously thinking of developing some creative theopolitical thought and praxis around the word kenarchy. Over the next few days I will explain why I like this word and I would of course very much welcome feedback!" So began the development of a whole new contemporary way of interacting with the Jesus narrative. Right from the start some people have found this word kenarchy difficult. Despite our making clear that it is a new, made-up word, many people reach for the dictionary and, not finding it there, struggle to take it seriously. Their understanding of theology is something static and received, and the very idea of changing core terminology is profoundly disturbing for them. So let us be clear right away here that the contributors to this book take the view that mature theological thought is developmental or, as

---

1. Arendt, *The Human Condition*, 214.

the apostle Paul put it, "from glory to glory."[2] We also take the view that social change, whether for good or ill, unavoidably impacts the way we understand words and sometimes it is necessary to adapt our use of language accordingly, otherwise meanings can change and in so doing displace or even negate their original content.

The greatest difficulty with the word kenarchy has been its starkly political nature. The second syllable, -*archy*, which means a way of ordering or relating in social space, connotes many other overtly political words like monarchy, anarchy, oligarchy, and, if you think about it, aristocracy, democracy, and so on. However, the whole idea that the gospel story is by nature political is very unpalatable for some people. Years ago I edited a student magazine for a Christian organization. There was a general election coming up and I invited representatives of the Labour and Conservative parties to contribute their viewpoint in the center-page spread. When the edition went before the organization's review panel before publication, the Labour contribution was censored for being too political despite setting out social policies clearly justified in terms of Jesus' prioritization of the poor. The Conservative one, it transpired, as far as the board was concerned, was not political at all! The status quo was simply perceived to be the norm. Tragically this is still the case for many people today. When they ask for religion to be kept out of politics, they really mean that it is about personal and private matters, and that it should not challenge the status quo. But it was precisely this that the use of the phrase "the kingdom of God" in the Jesus story was challenging head on. There was already a kingdom in place at the time, the empire of Rome, and Jesus' way and its way were shown to be utterly at odds with each other. The one saw peace coming through the exercise of hierarchical, sovereign power, while the other proclaimed peace through a humble lifestyle of kenotic love. In this context the good news of the kingdom of God was unequivocally a political message. By forming the word kenarchy to refer to the kingdom of God we are deliberately restoring the political character to the message of Jesus and reapplying it today. The message of

2. 2 Cor 3:18.

Jesus is a politics of peace, peace through love, but emphatically not a vague or vacuous love. Rather, it is a love measured by the distance necessary to cross in order to genuinely love one's enemy. As Jesus put it, in stark distinction from the politics of Rome and their Jewish puppet representatives who were in power at the time, "'The kings of the gentiles lord it over them . . . But it is not this way with you'"; instead, "love your enemies, do good to those who hate you."[3] Kenarchy, like the message of Jesus from which it is being developed, is first and foremost political. It is a deeply practical and contemporary politics of love.

It is not only those on the right wing who find difficulty with applying Jesus' message of love to the political realm. Some on the left find it equally problematic. The neo-Marxist philosopher Alain Badiou, in his book *In Praise of Love*, expresses the difficulty like this: "In my opinion, the politics of love is a meaningless expression. Principally because there are people in politics one doesn't love . . . that's undeniable, nobody can expect us to love them."[4] He goes on to identify "them" as one's enemies. He states, "The issue of the enemy is completely foreign to the question of love."[5] His fellow neo-Marxists Michael Hardt and Antonio Negri, on the other hand, make a counterbalancing plea for love as a politically revolutionary act. As they put it, "We need to recover today this material and political sense of love, a love as strong as death."[6] This book aims to answer those who separate love from politics and instead attempts to rediscover a politics of love, or kenarchy, that can provide a positive response to Michael Hardt and Antonio Negri's plea.

3. Luke 22:25–26; 6:27.
4. Badiou, *In Praise of Love*, 57.
5. Ibid., 59.
6. Hardt and Negri, *Multitude*, 352.

"THE POLITICS OF LOVE IS A MEANINGLESS EXPRESSION"

As we have seen, the negative reaction to the introduction of love into politics is so deeply rooted that both right-wing Christians and neo-Marxists have problems with it. Badiou's statement is part of a very revealing contemporary debate about the nature of politics that is heavily influenced by Carl Schmitt's configuration of the political. The German political philosopher died in 1985, but his work continues to resonate among those grappling with the deep political structures undergirding the Western world. Schmitt makes the friend-enemy distinction the defining political denominator. As he puts it, "the enemy is he who defines me."[7] Luke Bretherton takes this up in his paper *'Love Your Enemies': Usury, Citizenship and the Friend-Enemy Distinction* where he states, "Otherness for Schmitt represents a latent threat to one's own way of life because it represents a form of life that can replace or supersede one's own."[8]

There are two very significant issues to take note of consequent on Schmitt's configuration of sovereignty around the friend-enemy distinction. Firstly, his perspective mistakenly fuses sovereignty and politics together when they are not necessarily the same thing at all. Secondly, as a result, he displaces the love for "the other" such as expressed in Jesus' admonition to "love your enemies" from the political realm altogether.[9] Schmitt is fully aware of the implications of this, a complication that he resolves by pleading a highly unsatisfactory distinction between individual and corporate enemies. He states:

> The often quoted "Love your enemies" (Matt. 5:44; Luke 6:27) reads *diligite inimicos vestros*, . . . and not *diligite hostes vestros*. No mention is made of the political enemy . . . The enemy in the political sense need not be hated personally, and in the private sphere only does it make

7. Schmitt, *Theory of the Partisan*, 85.
8. Bretherton, "Love Your Enemies," 369.
9. Ibid., 360.

> sense to love one's enemy, i.e., one's adversary . . . It cer-
> tainly does not mean that one should love and support
> the enemies of one's own people.[10]

There is, however, no way that the gospel narratives sustain such a distinction between public and private enemies. It is rather the opposite. The context of Jesus' admonition to love, as contemporary research demonstrates, is of the political enmity of the puppet representatives of Rome towards him, and his move to appoint twelve apostles is full of political implications and symbols.[11] This displacement of the politics of love is part of what we can call a subsumption of politics by sovereignty, the genealogy of which reaches back to the fourth century and beyond. The previous book *The Fall of the Church* and the academic work undergirding it,[12] spells out the meaning and implications of this in some detail. Suffice it to say here that to subsume a thing is to hollow it out and fill it up with a different meaning and purpose such that its original function is lost and replaced with something else. It is a form of colonization, but applied to the deep structures of language and politics. As I have pointed out in the previous books, there is nothing new in Schmitt's subsumption of politics by sovereignty in this way, nor in Badiou's contemporary version of it. Their position is simply a postmodern continuation of a trajectory that supposes that the politics of sovereignty are the only means to peace, an assumption that has consistently and inevitably displaced the loving politics of Jesus. Schmitt's exegesis of the gospel narrative is simply a consequence of reading the gospel testimony through that all too resilient lens.

10. Schmitt, *The Concept of the Political*, 29.

11. Horsley, *Jesus and Empire*, 34.

12. Mitchell, *Church, Gospel, and Empire*.

THE DISPLACEMENT OF THE POLITICS OF LOVE BY THE POLITICS OF EMPIRE

The idea that the way to peace is necessarily via war is at face value a peculiarly contradictory one. But it has been a defining characteristic of Western political history since the partnership of church and empire in the days of Eusebius of Caesarea and the emperor Constantine.[13] The central assumption of this alignment was the conviction that the *pax Romana* was the positive fulfillment of a divine plan for universal peace developing via the empires of Greece and Rome on the one hand and the history of Israel and the church on the other.[14] The kind of politics that resulted enshrined the idea that peace could be enforced by a church-state partnership of hierarchical power at the center of what came to be called Christendom. As the Middle Ages passed into what is known as Modernity this partnership in power became an increasingly violent one as first the church, then the state, depending on whose power was greater at any given time, tried to exert its influence over the other. Neither the Enlightenment nor the Reformation solved the problem. Rather, the Enlightenment only tended to increase the conflict between church and state, and the Reformation added to it by introducing conflict between the Protestant, Catholic, and radical expressions of church. Far from resolving the conflict between church and state, the development of the modern nation state only shifted the politics of empire from the domination of a single overarching universal power to an uneasy co-existence between a multiplicity of states all attempting to keep the peace by exerting hierarchical forms of domination within and without. The apparent separation of powers that increasingly came to characterize the emerging Western representative democracy only served to conceal the continuing underlying assumption about the nature of power. In fact the modern Western nation state used the separation to maintain the dominance of sovereignty, and

13. For a comprehensive treatment of this perspective see Mitchell, *Church, Gospel, and Empire.*

14. Eusebius, *The History of the Church,* 39.

replaced the primary role of the church with the role of the market to the continued displacement of the politics of love.

This brief account of the genealogy of Western sovereignty helps explain the public/private separation where love for enemy is relegated to personal religion and private practice instead of shaping the political arena. It is in this context that the West continues to configure the political around violence and war with the inevitable conflictual outcome, and it is within this trajectory that Badiou and Schmitt can be seen to perpetuate a view of the political that renders the politics of love meaningless. In these circumstances it is only to be expected that the attempt to reintroduce a politics of love will tend to flounder unless it is accompanied by serious mindset change. As Paul Fletcher underlines, it involves an abandonment of the politically normal that is deeply "impolitical."[15] Nevertheless, the need to reconfigure a politics of love as the antidote to the necessarily violent and conflictual politics of sovereignty is arguably the most pressing need of our time.

RECONFIGURING A POLITICS OF LOVE

It is generally accepted that the Western world is now in a post-modern, post-Christendom era, a situation that has provoked a raft of responses both secular and religious.[16] Amongst these, as might be expected after nearly two millennia during which it has dominated the political landscape, the sovereignty-for-peace model remains intransigent and persistent. In this context kenarchy offers a serious countercultural alternative. Kenarchy empties out sovereign power and replaces it with a love measured by the readiness to die for "the other," even one's enemy. This re-emerging political resource for peace has four interrelated qualities: a relational approach to knowledge, a kenotic understanding of power, a clear sense of direction, and a subversive orientation towards the status quo.

15. Fletcher, *Disciplining the Divine*, 176.

16. See Murray Williams, *Post-Christendom*; see Mitchell, *The Fall of the Church*, Ch. 1.

(i) A relational approach to knowledge

The idea that knowledge is relational has major implications beyond the scope of this book. It does not imply that knowledge is not rational, but that rationality is dependent upon relationality. Kenarchy begins with a relational encounter with a loving other, akin to Badiou's construction of love as "an encounter" with what he calls "the quasi-metaphysical status of an *event,* namely of something that doesn't enter into the immediate order of things."[17] But whereas Badiou restricts this to a life that is being constructed "no longer from the perspective of One but from the perspective of Two,"[18] kenarchy begins with a reciprocal encounter with someone whose whole orientation is transformative of relationships beyond the personal to people as a whole. As has by now become clear, kenarchy has initially been configured mainly by those who have found the testimony to Jesus in the gospel narratives to be an archetypical fullness of such an encounter. For them it means that the sense of a distinctive difference to the immediate order leads to a fully metaphysical status for the event. A typical testimony to one such encounter from a south London teenager was, "Well, there's nothing special about you, but you have love, and seeing as how it can't come from you it must come from God." For others it will involve another faith source for love, and for yet others who are unable to apprehend divine transcendence, it will entail a kind of transcendence that remains, at least for the time being, on a human level. As Simon Critchley expresses it, "the latter requires an experience of faith, a faith of the faithless that is an openness to love, love as giving what one does not have and receiving that over which one has no power."[19] Whatever the case, the distinctive nature of the relationship is located in the kenotic quality of the love encountered. From the standpoint of Christian faith this kind of love belongs to what the gospel narratives call a son or daughter of peace, terminology that marks its inclusive nature, and

17. Badiou, *In Praise of Love,* 28.
18. Ibid., 29.
19. Critchley, *The Faith of the Faithless,* 7.

emphasizes that it is to be found elsewhere than only among those knowingly following Jesus.[20] Kenarchy proceeds from a reciprocal love relationship between any individuals whose love is kenotic towards each other personally and in the strength of which it reaches beyond to others generally.

(ii) A kenotic understanding of power

Kenarchy is properly described as kenotic, because it empties out power. However, it involves more than this. There are many different configurations of kenosis. But in the case of kenarchy it applies specifically to the emptying out of power motivated by love for "the other." It is the giving out of those gifts, abilities, qualities, and opportunities that a person has so that the loved other can flourish. Kenarchy begins with the reciprocal but it does not remain there. Rather it is measured not by love for the original lover, the one who loves back, but by love for one's enemies. It is a love that cannot and will not coerce, but encompasses the distance across which another, even one's enemies, can approach if they will. Oppositely to Schmitt's configuration of sovereignty, while the political remains defined by one's enemies, instead of those enemies being those that power seeks to subjugate, they become those that love inclusively encompasses. For this reason kenarchy looks for a body of reciprocal lovers or kenarchists who can encourage and support the exercise of self-giving when it is spurned or even violently rejected.

Kenarchy has as its defining characteristic the committed choice to embrace the ultimate symbol of the sovereign power of the exception. In the Roman Empire of Jesus' day this was the cross. Hence Jesus' admonition that anyone who would love like him needed to "take up his cross daily."[21] In the contemporary West this could be relegation to a non person, and being subjected to the water boarding and imprisonment without trial that has

20. Luke 10:6.
21. Luke 9:23.

been meted out to those in Guantanamo prison, the exile forced on Ed Snowden, or the thirty-five-year jail sentence given to Bradley Manning. It includes a readiness to be shot or bombed. This commitment only properly makes sense if it is realized in the hope of resurrection. In the context of the politics of Jesus, the resurrection is, as N. T. Wright has described, "*the* political act."[22] For it is the evidence of that love "greater than death" that Hardt and Negri look for, and proof that the politics of love works.

(iii) A clear sense of direction

Kenarchy is not a system or program, but a journey that begins with and continues to multiply loving connections by emptying out whatever power one has in the direction set by the original encounter and then extended in ongoing relationship. In terms of the shape of Jesus' politics this has at its heart seven specific foci: instating women, prioritizing children, advocating for the poor, welcoming the stranger, caring for the creation, freeing prisoners, and caring for the sick. It is clearly impossible to do all of this simultaneously, but it delineates a definite sense of direction and a practical manifesto for the exercise of kenotic love. It also has the effect of clarifying who are friends and who are enemies. These seven help to identify those friends whom I pour out kenotic love towards. Those individuals and institutions that deliberately or unconsciously oppress them are identified as enemies. These in turn provide a measure for the chasm of difference that needs to be crossed and the extent of love that is required for peace to be realized. A great deal of work is already being done by a whole variety of agencies to advocate for the seven categories above. Kenarchy recognizes that efforts to redress oppression have long been underway and gladly joins in, but its distinctive contribution is to empty out sovereign power on behalf of the oppressed and to subvert the powers that work against them. Many initiatives along

22. Ray Mayhew, "Turning the Tables, Resurrection as Revolution." Review of N. T. Wright, *The Resurrection of the Son of God*. No pages. Online: http://tinyurl.com/659lokn.

the trajectory of these seven foci fail to reject sovereign power as a means to peace. As a result the actions taken are at best limited in usefulness and at worse continue to perpetrate the problem even within the intended solution.

Kenarchy is love based, not law based, so it does not follow that the constant presence of need constitutes a legal demand or duty. Love begins with giving and receiving in mutual relationship and grows into a resource that can be shared. The general rule is to go with the flow of love, to be realistic about what is and is not possible, but to prefer risks to rationalizations. A simple but costly politics, kenarchy is organic, not organizational, viral not static, centrifugal not centripetal, and develops as an egalitarian distributive network of peers. It is something like the apostle Paul configured the church to be, if disentangled from overlaid forms of sovereign power.

(iv) A subversive orientation towards the status quo

Kenarchy is subversive of all sovereign power, particularly where it is abusive in terms of the foci outlined above. However, it operates from within the existing system in an attitude of love towards all involved. This is in the opposite spirit to the sovereignty approach which is so constructed as to exclude and if necessary destroy the enemy at the point when it becomes clear that they will not adapt to the defining deep-structural norms of the prevailing group. Kenarchy, however, configures the enemy inclusively as "the ones we love." This applies both to the individual enemy or a whole people group. It is not a question of loving the system, but those individuals and groups who uphold it. For this reason kenarchy does not seek to immediately overturn the offending institution that it confronts. Instead it seeks to overcome it by degrees in a loving rhythm of subversion and submission.

Given that kenarchy is of a qualitatively different order to sovereignty and that its direction is supportive of those groups that the system tends to oppress, those who practice kenarchy soon find themselves provoked to acts of subversive behavior in opposition to the status quo. But after emptying out whatever power they can to subvert the system for human flourishing, they then, as known subversives, nonetheless submit to the system until another appropriate time. The aim is to subvert the status quo with a new kind of power[23] that is then infused into the already constituted power by radical submission that awaits the next opportunity for a new love-based subversion. By means of this rhythm it is possible to build new love-motivated institutions as well as transforming existing ones. Through the same process it is also possible to subvert these if they default back to sovereign power. It is the failure to recognize this rhythm in the politics of Jesus and his followers that has led to the misunderstanding of Jesus' admonition to "render to Caesar the things that are Caesar's"[24] and Paul's and Peter's advice to submit to "the powers that be."[25] Far from Jesus and his followers advocating uncritical support of the status quo, the narratives make clear that they first challenged the very roots of the authority of the prevailing political power, and only after the inevitable upheaval did they then advocate submission. It is precisely this rhythm that kenarchy emulates.

Timing plays a very important part in the outworking of kenarchy. It is initiated by an event in time, and so timing plays a vital part in how it proceeds. The peace through sovereignty model carries with it a controlling sense of time where the fullness of the future peace is continuously delayed. Kenarchy on the other hand reconceives time as a series of personal and corporate outbreaks of subversive experiences of present peace that become the resource from which the social order can be progressively transformed. Initiating such events on behalf of the oppressed and against the powers calls for wisdom, humor, music, the arts, learning by risk, mistakes, experiences, collaboration, prayer, and other spiritual exercises.

23. The theorists call this constituent power.
24. Matt 22:21–22. Cf. Matt 21:12–13.
25. Rom 13:1; 1 Pet 2:13. Cf. Acts 4:19–20; 23:1–3.

"LOVE AS A POLITICAL ACT THAT CONSTRUCTS THE MULTITUDE"

Hardt and Negri, in their two books *Empire* and *Multitude*, explain the contemporary Western political system in terms of biopower. In accord with Foucault and others they make clear that human life itself, or what they describe as "naked life," is now the primary raw material of postmodern capitalism. Hardt and Negri underline the way that this development has been accompanied by an IT revolution that has transformed labor power into immaterial labor, or what Paolo Virno calls potential power because its use of the worldwide web and social networking provides the opportunity to subvert the commercial and political process.[26] It is their hope that this potential power has the capacity to revolutionize politics by empowering the multitude. However, the totalizing hegemony of biopower is so all-pervasive that any such breakthrough of potential power requires a completely different kind of power to activate the people. Their hope is for a recovery of the love that originally motivated the Judaeo-Christian tradition. As they put it, "Christianity and Judaism . . . both conceive love as a political act that constructs the multitude . . . We need to recover today this material and political sense of love, a love as strong as death."[27] The reorientation towards kenotic power provided by kenarchy, measured by the distance to one's enemy and marked by the embrace of the place of the exception to the point of death, has the potential to motivate this new social solidarity characterized by love.

It is no doubt clear by now that the discovery and formation of kenarchy is a huge task that is only in its very early stages. In the ensuing chapters, rather than setting out a program or presenting a prescriptive or definitive practice that would give the lie to the inclusive relational nature of kenarchy, we have two main goals. Firstly, to expose the particular nature of kenotic love that provides the heartbeat of kenarchy, and, secondly, to explore the holistic application of kenarchy throughout some of the main occupational

26. Virno, *The Grammar of the Multitude*, 82.
27. Hardt and Negri, *Multitude*, 352.

spheres, concerns, and component parts of contemporary society. Part of the orientation of kenarchy is to seek out and draw on kenotic resources for love wherever they can be found. There are significant resources to be mined in the core writings of other faiths, as well as among secular thinkers. Kenarchy's inclusive approach energizes an open dialogue that the politics of sovereignty tends to preclude. While an important undertaking, this too is clearly a massive one! It is hoped that the chapters that follow will serve to earth the practical potential of kenarchy as contemporary radical politics and provide some of the necessary motivation to continue this exciting work.

1

The Heart of Love

Roger Haydon Mitchell

THERE IS NO MORE toxic example of how the sovereignty model of power has misconstrued the Jesus story than the penal substitution theory of what was happening at the cross. It presents God as the ultimate offended sovereign authority requiring appeasement of his "righteous" anger at those who fail to do what he wants. This is the opposite of a love that does not insist on its own way,[1] and effectively recasts God in the image of the sinner. As Richard Rohr has so tellingly put it, "in order to turn Jesus into a Hero we ended up making the Father into a 'Nero.'"[2] While the satisfaction theories tone this down by making the problem more relational and less forensic, they still cast God in the role of the offended lawmaker rather than the lover who resolves the painful consequences of rejection in their own heart instead of visiting it on some substitute victim. But it is the latter that so often remains the defining perspective of the cross and shows itself in

1. Cf. 1 Cor 13:5.
2. Rohr, "The Franciscan Opinion," 208.

16

many traditional understandings of the Roman Catholic mass, the Protestant communion, and the portrayal of the gospel in much so-called Christian evangelism. Jesus "loved me and gave Himself up for me"[3] is understood in the limited sense of Jesus taking my legally required punishment instead of me. As Rohr again sees so perceptively, the great danger of this is that we are distracted from discipleship into worship. "We end up worshipping Jesus as a quasi-substitute for following him, which is of course what he actually proposed."[4]

The *Christus Viktor* theology of the cross, characteristic of the Orthodox Churches of the East, which has recently been given new exposure by theologians such as Greg Boyd, is more palatable because, to some extent, it shifts the focus of the atonement away from the Father.[5] Here the problem is seen to be more with evil and Satan, than with an offended God, and the emphasis is on the demonic nature of the powers, and the cross as the location in time where their aggression against the human race was exhausted. However, while the *Christus Viktor* approach does emphasize the importance of love in overcoming evil, it still leaves the sovereignty model intact, or at least in part unchallenged. The end result is the substitution of one Lordship for another, a good Lord for a bad Lord, rather than one who upends lordship altogether.

It is the intention of this chapter to reframe the meaning of the life, death, and resurrection of Jesus in the light of the gospel narratives and away from the sovereignty approach altogether. This is because kenarchy has at its heart a completely opposite understanding of authority to that of empire and regards the latter's foundational characteristics as destructive. In line with this, rather than embarking on an examination of atonement theories applied to God or the devil, this chapter looks at developments in non-violent theology and draws on them to fully connect the incarnation with the cross and reveal the authority of love that is at the heart of kenarchy.

3. Gal 2:20.
4. Rohr, "The Franciscan Opinion," 208, note 4.
5. See Boyd, "The Christus Victor View," 23–49.

NON-VIOLENT THEOLOGY FOR A NON-VIOLENT POLITICS

Among others, René Girard, Simone Weil, Thomas Torrance, and Miroslav Volf provide important examples in their work of the way that theology has progressed towards a recovery of Jesus' understanding of the cross as encountered in the gospel narratives. Drawing on these innovative theologies the chapter attempts to frame a practical kenarchic perspective of the incarnation and cross as the means to expose and overcome the binary "them and us" of empire, and forerun a new humanity who will give themselves away as the humble exemplars and saviors of the multitude.

(i) The mimetic theory of René Girard

One of the most influential theological developments of the past few decades is the mimetic theory devised by the French Catholic theologian René Girard, who has done important work in positioning the cross as the culmination and reversal of a theme of sacrifice common to the ancient religions of Hinduism and Buddhism, as well as Judaism. He states, "If the term *sacrifice* is used for the death of Jesus, it is in a sense absolutely contrary to the archaic sense. Jesus consents to die in order to reveal the lie of blood sacrifices and to render them henceforth impossible."[6] This understanding of the cross provides the antidote to those atonement theories that ignore the Old Testament castigation of child sacrifice and make God the ultimate child sacrificer. Instead, Girard demonstrates that sacrifice has developed a central role through human history by means of a process of mimetic rivalry in which the multitude or human mob forms two or more sides which become embroiled in a violent conflict that is finally, but not in the end permanently, resolved by the sacrifice of a scapegoat victim that is given the blame for the enmity. He argues that the sacrifice of Jesus brings this to an end because he is an utterly innocent victim who voluntarily substitutes himself for the scapegoat

6. Girard, *Sacrifice*, xi.

victim. Instead of substantiating and only temporarily resolving the mimetic rivalry, in the manner of the normal scapegoat victim, Jesus' deliberate and voluntary sacrifice replaces rivalry with love and makes permanent reconciliation possible.

This has the great benefit of interpreting the cross in terms of kenotic love instead of making it a resolution of the rivalry for power that lies at the base of sovereignty. However, it still appears to leave the blame for the original violence as a property of the mob. "The mimeticism appears foremost in the mob and in the imitation of the mob to which all the spectators of the crucifixion surrender."[7] So while he goes a long way towards disconnecting the cross from sovereign power and configuring it in a kenotic direction, Girard's mimetic theory still stops short of making the exposure of the hierarchical abuse of power central to the good news. But this does not equate with Jesus' compassionate affirmation of the multitude that clearly places the responsibility for their being "distressed and dispirited like sheep without a shepherd" firmly at the door of the shepherds, the religious and political leaders of Israel and Rome.[8]

(ii) Simone Weil and the domination of the will

Some of Simone Weil's profound insights can help us here, with her identification of the roots of violent rivalry in the "darkness" that she identifies as the will, or "willing through mastery."[9] This takes us on from a general guilt of the multitude for the mimetic scapegoating process to a specific locus of responsibility in those who exercise the will to power. Once it is understood that Weil uses "will" in an altogether negative sense as the selfish will to power, something at least similar to, if not identical to sovereignty, her insights can take us a step further in identifying the purpose of the cross and thereby the incarnation which it culminates. For

7. Ibid., 67.
8. Matt 9:36.
9. Jersak, "We Are Not Our Own," 72.

her the cross is the place where Jesus surrendered his will for the sake of love. This goes to the heart of kenarchy. At the cross God surrenders any legitimate claim to sovereign power for the sake of love. As she puts it, "the abandonment at the supreme moment of the crucifixion, what an abyss of love on both sides."[10]

While Weil's profound understanding of love as the emptying out of the will to mastery basic to sovereign power takes us to the heart of the matter, she has a frustrating tendency to regard the will itself as evil. It seems that there is a paradox for her in the existence of evil, or what she describes as necessity, that reveals both the glory of what it is to be divine and the desolation of what it is to be human. For her there is something inescapable about the human condition that God has to traverse the "infinite thickness of"[11] in order to be God, but also embrace the God-forsakenness of, in order to experience the fullness of what it is to be human. Weil perceives the will to be responsible for this God-forsaken suffering. Hence, for her, the will needs to be more than surrendered, it needs to be eradicated.[12] This is rooted, perhaps, in her avowed Platonism, with its essential hierarchy of the spiritual over the material, or it may be that something unresolved in her experience of life moved her to embrace a seemingly unbridgeable gap between God and humanity that only violent suffering could span.

Whatever the reason, instead of recognizing a positive will to love as a qualitatively different kind of power to the will to mastery, Weil seems, at times, in danger of making the cross a place of obliteration of the wills rather than the revelation and consummation of the will to love. This kind of kenosis extends self-emptying to the very depths of identity and is, at best, in danger of falling into the trap identified by Rohr, where we mistake worship-inducing profundity for practical discipleship. At worst, it hides the possibility of something within the nature of what it is to be both divine and human that substantiates the destructive power of empire, instead of the life-affirming gift of mutual love. The latter must surely

10. Weil, *Gravity and Grace*, 87.
11. Ibid., 90.
12. Jersak, "We Are Not Our Own," 85.

involve a wholesome exercise of the will, and to claim otherwise lessens the full implications of incarnation. This positive use of the will in the choice to give ourselves is expressed in Jesus' words "not my will, but Yours be done."[13] And of course, if Jesus reveals God, then his choice to submit his will to another encapsulates the essence of the kenosis at the heart of God and is the very opposite of the sovereignty system that bends and obliterates the freedom of "the other." Divinity yields to love for "the other," including one's enemies, as is manifest in Jesus' life, and so can we. The will to mastery can be surrendered and replaced by the will to love.

(iii) Thomas Torrance and Jesus' vicarious humanity

Thomas Torrance advances an exciting perspective that takes us way beyond any need to obliterate the will through suffering by making the whole incarnation an alternative to the human will to mastery and the gift of what he describes as Jesus' vicarious humanity. This renders all of Jesus' life a substantial resource on which to draw in place of the will to mastery with its destructive behaviors and responses. As Torrance puts it, "It was for our sakes and in our place that Jesus lived that vicarious life in utter reliance upon God and in laying hold upon his mercy and goodness."[14] This opens up the kingdom of heaven to everyone in accord with Jesus' words from Matthew, "Not everyone who says to Me, 'Lord, Lord,' will enter the kingdom of heaven, but he who does the will of My Father who is in heaven will enter."[15] Instead of presenting God as a dominating sovereign requiring appeasement, it presents God freely giving his will to love, to us, as a gift for fully human living. Something the apostle Paul describes as making a new humanity.[16]

There is, however, in my view, an ambiguity with Torrance's position, in that his strong emphasis on God's grace means that

13. Luke 22:42.

14. Torrance, *Incarnation*, 125.

15. Matt 7:21.

16. Eph 2:15.

he underrates the role of human freedom in response to the extraordinary gift of Jesus' kenarchic life. As Jeff McSwain positively affirms, the quality of human being represented by Christ's vicarious humanity excludes the opportunity "for men and women to respond from a center in themselves, external to Christ, instead of from within the incarnational union established by Christ the Spirit."[17] The problem with this is that it appears to make the divine provision another form of mastery, even if a positive one. As a result Torrance states rather starkly, "any Christological approach that starts from the man Jesus, from the historical Jesus, and tries to pass over to God, and so to link human nature to God, is utterly impossible."[18] So while the vicarious humanity of Christ links the divine and the human, Torrance's view of grace necessitates that the initiative must all lie with God. The problem is that any approach that makes a qualitative distinction between divinity and humanity rather than a quantitative one provides a potential legitimation of similar hierarchical separations between one human and another. The whole mystery of the incarnation is that it bridges that gap.

It is the purpose of this book to configure the politics of love that so many have encountered in the Jesus story. So while it is not the intention to assume confessional agreement about the incarnation of Jesus, it would have profound implications if the story of Jesus left open the possibility of a necessary qualitative distinction between divinity and humanity, even for the purposes of emphasizing divine grace. For it has been precisely the assumed hierarchical relationship between God and humanity that has been used to justify the hierarchical political forms of the sovereignty system. It is not being asserted here that the New Testament narratives of Jesus' life provide a controlling statement of rationalistic truth, but it is being suggested that they provide a reasonable record of affectively convincing historically based accounts of the life of the human from Nazareth sufficient for the exercise of faith for those who desire it. This is affirmed by the helpful hermeneutics

17. McSwain, *Movements of Grace*, 6.

18. Torrance, *Incarnation*, 10.

of differently positioned complementary theologians such as N. T. Wright with his critical realism, or Graham Ward with his economy of response, as I describe in Part III of *Church, Gospel, and Empire*. However, despite what is, in my view, a flaw in Torrance's position, he skillfully choreographs the Jesus story as the score by which the divine life is made comprehensively available and liveable, for all would-be people of peace. It is this accessible, tangible quality of the incarnation that provides the substance of kenarchy.

(iv) Miroslav Volf and the will to embrace

The evocative image of Jesus on the cross, his arms outstretched to encompass the whole human race in his loving life, death, and resurrection, is the summation of the incarnation in the context of sovereign power. This is kenarchy embodied; this is what the freely available humanity of Christ looks like. Miroslav Volf, drawing on Paul's statement, "God demonstrates His own love toward us, in that while we were yet sinners, Christ died for us,"[19] describes this as indiscriminate love. As he puts it, "On the cross, God is manifest . . . as the God of indiscriminate love who died for the ungodly to bring them into the divine communion."[20] He goes on to describe this kind of love for "the other" as "the will to embrace," a term that positions it as the complete opposite of what Weil describes as the will to mastery. This definition of love as the will to embrace takes us another step forward in configuring the politics of kenarchy that proceeds from the Jesus story.

Volf presents four crucial components. Firstly, his configuration of love rejects the construction of the world around exclusive moral polarities. The will to embrace transcends any moral/immoral, legal/illegal, good/evil, right/wrong, binary distinctions. Whoever is involved, and whatever allegations are being made, the outstretched arms of love desire to encompass them all. Secondly, he makes clear that this kind of love most definitely includes

19. Rom 5:8.
20. Volf, "Forgiveness, Reconciliation and Justice," 280.

serious attention to issues of justice. It is not about affirming or ignoring the abuse of power by either party, because "an embrace that neither play-acts acceptance nor crushes the other, cannot take place until justice is attended to."[21] However, this is emphatically not a shift back to love being conditional on binary polarities. As Volf explains, it is not about requiring any kind of strict justice within pre-decided, prescriptive terms. Rather, "It is a way of creating a genuinely and deeply human community of harmonious peace in an imperfect world of inescapable injustice." In other words, because the whole domination system is unjust at source, a wholly new positive means to peace is being offered. Thirdly, the loving will to embrace initiates this new community of humanity because it carries a passion to include "the other," something Volf calls "the light of knowledge."[22] It orientates the heart to see through the eyes of "the other" and to illuminate any desire for good residing there. Finally, the will to embrace provides the ultimate horizon and purpose of the struggle for peace and justice. It is not about people getting what they deserve, but the "larger goal of healing relationships."

While this exposition of the will to embrace certainly carries us further into the heart of kenarchy, it still stops short of the full story. For while Volf understands the will to embrace to be completely indiscriminate, and therefore the first step on the road to forgiveness, he excludes the possibility of complete forgiveness by the victim without the repentance of the perpetrator. He argues that a will to embrace that includes justice and offers forgiveness, will at the same time "condemn the deed and accuse the doer," and that to receive forgiveness will at the same time "admit the deed and accept the blame."[23] He concludes therefore that "an unrepentant wrongdoer must in the end remain an unforgiven wrongdoer— the unconditionality of the first step in the process of forgiveness notwithstanding."[24] Now while recognizing with Volf that

21. Ibid., 281.
22. Ibid., 282.
23. Ibid., 283.
24. Ibid., 284.

mutual reconciliation and the attainment of a common life cannot be achieved without repentance, and notwithstanding the text of Luke's account of Jesus' encouragement to forgive the person who sins against you and says "I repent" seven times in one day, it is not enough.[25] Jesus' words are not by way of a neo-legalistic statement to limit love, but rather the vehicle to carry us to their loving culmination. In any case if someone sins against the same person seven times in a day (Matthew has seventy times seven) and still claims to be repentant, it is grounds for questioning how seriously they are taking the whole thing! The story is surely referring to forgiving the, at least, relatively unrepentant. No, if the cross does not go all the way to forgive the unrepentant we have a huge problem. We have no means to live in positive peace with our real enemies unless they effectively become our friends, and many of them will not.

THE AUTHORITY OF LOVE

This final section of the chapter attempts three things. Firstly, it contends that the love at the heart of kenarchy really does encompass our enemies, whether or not they are repentant. Secondly, it emphasizes that the very nature, or what theologians call the ontology, of the power of love is qualitatively different to the power of sovereignty. Thirdly, it recognizes that there is a serious tendency to default back to sovereign power that can interfere with our attempts at kenarchic politics and that requires constant reflection and humility if it is to be avoided.

(i) Love that encompasses our enemies

It is the certainty that not all our enemies will become our friends that leads Badiou and others to the conclusion that a politics of love must be impossible, as we saw in the Introduction. But the kenarchic view of the cross takes us beyond this problem because it regards the cross as a primary event in time where the

25. Luke 17:4.

outpouring of kenotic love, that culminates there, ingests the full effects of unrepentance. The destruction of human life that is the inevitable cost of the survival of the sovereignty system is met by a love stronger than death. When the unrepentant were killing Jesus, he was crying out, "Father, forgive them; for they do not know what they are doing,"[26] and his willing embrace of the execution with which they rejected his love ultimately overcame their unforgiveness and injustice by rendering it powerless in the face of his resurrection. The non-violent God and his new humanity embrace a cross, not because of any desire to punish, avenge, or be appeased, but because there needs to be a place to which all the violent and destructive consequences of empire and enmity can be diverted and exhausted while at the same time the embrace of love continues to encompass everyone, including the most implacable enemy. The cross is thus seen as the place where the non-violent God, embodied in a non-violent humanity, willingly takes the worst violence and injustice consequent on selfish human choices and deposits them in the depths of their own being. To put it another way, the cross is a gateway into a cosmic cesspit, or in Jesus' terms a Gehenna, where the destructive pain and suffering of ongoing enmity can be contained in the eternal now, and are forever overwhelmed by, but cannot overwhelm, the love that is there. A new humanity, now no longer simply in the divine image but in fellowship with the persons of the divinity and one another, now have access to that same overwhelming kenarchy and can in the same way love their enemies while diverting the effluent of enmity into the nucleus of love. Now in solidarity with us, far from condemning them for their behavior, God continues to appeal to the enemies of love and peace to be reconciled. The willing embrace of our enemies ultimately triumphs. This is the utterly different kind of authority to sovereignty that amazed the multitude.[27]

Of course repentance is necessary to be an effective part of the kenarchic company. If love's embrace is forced it is not love. You cannot make somebody love you, no matter how much you

26. Luke 23:34.
27. Matt 7:28–29; John 7:46.

love them. In sexual terms that is rape. Love forced is psychological and political rape. The invitation to repent (from the Greek *metanoia*: to change one's mind and behavior) has to be accepted before a person can be an active partner in a community that loves its enemies. But repentance is not necessary in order to be loved and forgiven by such a community. Otherwise loving my enemy becomes meaningless. The point is not that my enemy is my friend or my co-worker in the cause of kenarchy, but the one I love. The loving society may not be universal, but love is. It is crucially important to grasp this, because otherwise the gap between God and humanity, and between humans, that we have already noted, re-emerges, and the friend/enemy distinction lying at the basis of sovereignty, remains in place, and we are back where we started. Unless the cross can be shown to substantiate a love that actually does incorporate our enemies, then kenarchy has nothing truly revolutionary to offer. If it can, then kenarchy really is good news.

(ii) Qualitatively different kinds of power

It should by now be becoming clear that this recurring question of the possibility of a qualitative gap between the human and the divine is more than a theoretical one. It is a key to the deep structural political problem that has beset theology, politics, and personal behavior for centuries because it has the potential to justify ongoing injustice and oppression. Behind it is the question of the nature of power. If power itself necessarily functions in terms of hierarchical domination, where those with the greatest capacity to get their own way dominate the rest, then in the end might is right. The issues of morality and the common good are decided by those in the positions of power. So even if those in positions of power act in ways that appear to promote love and the common good, that goodness is still predicated on sovereign power, and if the latter is threatened the former will be displaced by the state of the exception and the system will be defended with the violence that is its necessary means to supposed peace and security. The deciding factor is sovereign power. If, however, power is not necessarily sovereign at all, but there are qualitatively, not just quantitatively different expressions of power, then another way of relating to each other is open to us. As the Introduction has made clear, the research behind this book concludes that our understanding of power has been subsumed by sovereignty, and that as a result our Western world has developed around the notion that this kind of power is the only way to peace. This is the opposite of the politics of Jesus, which embodies and proclaims the power of love.

In this current series of books it has been the practice to use the word power in a neutral way, but the word sovereignty in a wholly negative way. In this usage, power can refer to *either* the power of love *or* the sovereign power of the dominant world system, whereas sovereign power refers exclusively to those configurations of power that assume that the way to peace is through hierarchical domination by an individual or group, including the apparently democratically elected representatives of an "electorate" or government of the "People." However, the core proposal of kenarchy is that the exercise of ultimate power over others is never legitimate at all and that the politics of Jesus demonstrates an authority that is configured in terms of a self-giving love that is never over others, but always among or alongside them. This is not at all to say that there are no limited, temporary situations where a hierarchical order of operation may be submitted to the power of love necessary to achieve a specific and clearly limited end, such as training a child, flying a plane, or conducting a delicate operation. In these cases the purpose will be to get to the normal, mature situation of gift collaboration among loving equals as soon as possible. But it has to be recognized that such situations are fraught with danger, and constant vigilance is required to prevent these limited hierarchical forms from defaulting back to sovereignty.

(iii) Default interference

The genealogy of sovereignty is so strong, and runs so deep in the Western psyche, that without a determined, reflective commitment to the politics of kenarchy, it continually resurges in the lives of individuals and social groups. This is hardly surprising because we are not talking about a past historical system but a current and dominant power structure in which we live out our daily lives and which impacts every area of them. As the Introduction has intimated, we are living in an age of biopower where our very life is the raw material of sovereign power. It is not for nothing that Foucault calls this the society of control.[28] The whole social, economic, and political edifice of human existence is speaking sovereign power into us all the time. Kenarchy does not remove us into an alternative world or utopian ghetto, but rather lives out a subversive rhythm in the present world of sovereign power. However, precisely because kenarchy empties out the sovereign power that we have within the system to those who are relatively powerless in sovereign terms, it is constantly dealing with the power plays of hierarchy. Unless the qualitatively different kind of power that kenarchy configures, is constantly renewed as the motivation for these interplays, empire can all too easily rear its sovereign head in us again and we will find ourselves regarding the powerless as really so, and us as their benefactors. Actually, unless we do empty out what power we have at the appropriate times, then we ourselves are found again to be the perpetrators and supporters of the system. If we are not really sure that the power of love can overcome the power of sovereignty, then we will be unable to break the personal and corporate subconscious assumption that real power is sovereign, either positively by our own decisions or negatively in our reactions to experiences that have impacted our own sense of identity. This is an intensely practical matter. Even when we are consciously aware of the political context and deliberately choosing the power of love instead, the mental, social, and physical oppression of the sovereignty system in our own lives can leave us with serious reactive interference that affects our thinking, our decision-making, and our behavior. We need deep relationships with fellow loving human beings to coach, challenge, and encourage us to continually choose the potential power of love.

28. Foucault, *The History of Sexuality*, 140.

2

The Instatement of Women

Exploring Women's Position as Victim and Perpetrator

Julie Tomlin Arram

"THE TIME IS COMING when not only men but women will prophesy; not only aged men but young men, not only superiors, but inferiors, not only those that have university learning but those who have it not, even servants and handmaids."[1]

The history of women's struggle for equality in the West often focuses on the Suffragette movement of the late nineteenth and early twentieth centuries, or the more recent "second wave" feminism of the 1960s and 1970s. The words above, however, spoken by Mary Cappe in 1645, point to women's participation in "a whole raft of radical experiments away from the currency of empire" that took place in the middle of the seventeenth century.[2]

1. Rowbotham, *Hidden from History*, 13.
2. Mitchell, *The Fall of the Church*, 53.

Inspiration for many of these experiments was found in Puritan beliefs that challenged the excesses of the established church, emphasizing the importance of the inner spirit or conscience and asserting that man could communicate directly with God. While these beliefs brought to the surface fundamental questions about the very structure of Western society and the relationship between God, people, and land, they also inspired radical Puritans to challenge patriarchy when they took ideas like the rights of conscience of all believers to their logical conclusion: male ownership of wives and daughters was challenged, women were included in the decision-making of some of the small Puritan sects, and the prohibition on women preaching was lifted.[3]

At around the same time in Puritan New England, a new figure of womanhood began to emerge during a period of conflict with the Native Americans. More than 1,600 settlers were seized in raids that took place between King Philip's War, or Metacom's War, in 1675 and the end of the French and Indian War in 1763.[4] The image of "Judaea Capta" emerged during this period in the sermons of Cotton Mather, a minister who took the image embossed on the coin of a woman leaning on a palm tree, originally thought to represent Jerusalem, and likened it to the trials of the settlers. This depiction of the community in feminine terms and the belief that captivity for both sexes represented a divinely granted opportunity gave rise to the publication of female captivity narratives by the church-controlled printing presses. This was a remarkable development, not only because it enabled women to speak directly about their own experiences, but because it led Puritans to champion "a vision of femininity in which the rigors of the frontier were confronted by a woman who, however humble and dependent on God, was active, enterprising and rigorous in her pursuit of that humility and dependency."[5]

3. Rowbotham, *Hidden from History*, 9–10.
4. Faludi, *The Terror Dream*, 209.
5. Ibid., 221.

The first and most famous of the captivity narratives was written by Mary Rowlandson, a minister's wife who was captured in February 1675.[6]

Women and men remained unequal socially, but Rowlandson's 1682 narrative expressed precisely the idea of captivity as an opportunity to struggle towards submission to God in which both men and women could participate:

> but now I see the Lord has his time to scourge and chasten me. The portion of some is to have their Affliction by drops, now one drop and then another: but the dregs of the Cup, the wine of astonishment, like a sweeping rain that leaveth no food, did the Lord prepare to be my portion . . .

> And I hope I can say in some measure, as David did, It is good for me that I have been afflicted. The Lord hath shewed me . . . that we must rely on God himself, and our whole dependence must be upon him.[7]

In the case of Hannah Duston, who was captured after being left in the house with her newborn baby while her husband escaped with their other children, Faludi shows how the church community struggled to assimilate the stories and shape them to the Judaea Capta motif. The particular problem Duston's story posed was that she not only escaped, she killed a number of her captors and returned home with their scalps. The minister Cotton Mather invoked the story of Jael, who by killing the enemy general, Sisera, with a tent peg and mallet, helped deliver Israel, accompanied with the warning that "if you continue Unhumbled in your Sins, you will be the Slaves of Devils."[8] Puritan beliefs about the purpose of captivity opened up a space in which a "culturally central and individually strong" woman—or stalwart—could begin to take shape.[9] But growing fear that instead of awaiting God's

6. Ibid., 208.
7. Ibid., 218.
8. Ibid., 227.
9. Ibid., 238.

intervention women were taking control of their destinies, led to a backlash and the gradual introduction of narratives that portrayed women as a "figure of a hysterical, marginal dependent requiring male salvation."[10]

WOMEN AS SOVEREIGN SUBJECTS

The way in which the portrayal of womanhood changed to suit the needs of the religious and political authorities as the war with the Native Americans escalated suggests that the Puritan era is an important one to explore in relation to sovereignty. It sheds light on how the church and ruling authorities often colluded, at times with extreme violence, to exert control over the liberating potential of faith and impose a model of femininity that suited economic and political imperatives of the time. In the witch hunts that took place in America in the last decades of the seventeenth century, in which Mather played a prominent role, the common thread that ran through the sins witches were charged with was "female pride" and a "lack of deference,"[11] Faludi shows. In Europe, the witch hunts represented a two-hundred-year campaign of terror against "women's resistance to the spread of capitalist relations and the power that women had gained by virtue of their sexuality, their control over reproduction, and their ability to heal."[12] By the time the witch hunts ended, women had been expelled from the workplace and the figure of the housewife whose main focus was the home had been created.

The specter of the witch hunt was also used by the ruling elites to demonize indigenous peoples of the colonies, and later, in 1871, the women supporters of the short-lived Paris Commune, suggesting that the creation of scapegoats is a powerful weapon in the armory of sovereignty. In fact, modern-day witch hunts, such as those that took place in parts of Africa in the latter part of the

10. Ibid., 238.
11. Ibid., 234.
12. Federici, *Caliban and the Witch*, 239.

twentieth century, are a sure-fire sign that "the privatization of land and other communal resources, mass impoverishment, plunder, and the sowing of division in once-cohesive communities" are once again on the agenda, Federici claims.[13]

THE CHALLENGE OF WOMEN'S POSITION WITHIN IMPERIALISM

There is another important aspect of the Judaea Capta story, and that is that the story of the stalwart woman emerged during a time of violent conflict that ultimately led to the conquest and appropriation of land owned by the Native Americans. The unique position of white Western women in relation to sovereign power that this suggests was also evident in the Suffragette movement that emerged in the nineteenth century. While they secured the vote for all women over the age of twenty-one by 1928, the Suffragettes were not opposed to capitalism, and their agenda remained very much aligned to Britain's imperial interests. The belief in the superiority of European societies and the racial, religious, and cultural inferiority of all non-European subjects that drove the subjugation of the colonies also inspired a zeal to save women from oppression in those societies in the last decades of the nineteenth century.

"This narrative was useful in this era of European imperialism in that it encased European man in the role as colonizer as someone who, by virtue of his imperialist rule, was not only bringing civilization to backward peoples but also saving local women from the oppression and degradation imposed on them by native men."[14]

The belief that European women were inferior to men remained, however: while serving as Consul General in Egypt from 1883 to 1907, Evelyn Baring, a member of the powerful Baring family, waged a vocal campaign against the veil, which he believed exemplified Islam's "degradation" of women. Yet he was also a formidable opponent of English women's right to vote, serving as

13. Ibid., 170.
14 Ahmed, *A Quiet Revolution*, 23.

President of the Society Opposed to Women's Suffrage, which he said would undermine the family and position of men, with disastrous consequences for England and Empire.[15] Rather than challenge European imperial notions of superiority, however, women legitimized its "warped logic" by casting their movement as yet another product of a superior civilization that Britain exported, argues Antoinette Burton: "Feminist writers who constructed arguments for the need for female emancipation built them around the spectre of a passive and enslaved Indian womanhood. As a result, a colonial female Other was one of the conceptual foundations of Victorian feminist thinking."[16]

Half a century later, in the 1960s and 1970s, many women did challenge imperialism as part of a "second wave" of feminism, which Nancy Fraser argues "appeared as part of a broader emancipatory project, in which struggles against gender injustices were necessarily linked to the struggles against racism, imperialism, homophobia, and class domination, all of which required transformation of the deep structures of society."[17] This project remained "largely stillborn" as a result of historical forces, which she says "with the benefit of hindsight" included the shift from state-organized capitalism to an era of neo-liberalism. Charting feminism's abandonment of its critique of capitalism and transformation into a variant of identity politics in its third wave of the 1990s, Fraser makes an important distinction between a social movement committed to gender justice and a "general discursive construct" that feminists no longer own or control that has become an "empty signifier" in the same way that many argue the term "democracy" has.[18]

---

15. Ibid., 31.
16. Burton, *Burdens of History*, 63.
17. Fraser, *The Fortunes of Feminism*, 217.
18. Ibid., 224.

MAKING THE PERSONAL POLITICAL

This is an important development to bear in mind as we turn to how a kenarchic, love-based politics might contribute to the development of a feminist emancipatory project that acknowledges the achievements of the past, while seeking to overthrow imperial, sovereign aspects of that same history. Such an approach draws on, and engages with, current feminist thinking about identity and agency in the context of a transformatory politics. It also engages with a "fourth wave" of digital feminism and the opportunities it affords for grassroots networks in a globalized context as the internet and worldwide web becomes an increasingly important space for activists.

(i) Extending to the "abjected" margins

Firstly, it is important to identify who in today's neo-liberal context constitutes the marginalized "other" as we "scope out" the direction of kenarchy. It is vital that we develop a framework in which love-based action extends to those who, as Imogen Tyler demonstrates, have been made "national abjects" to do the "dirty ideological work of neoliberalism"[19] – among them women migrants in detention and facing deportation, Gypsies and Travellers, the young and disabled.[20]

Finishing this chapter on a day when the UK Independence Party is one of a number of anti-immigration parties across Europe to have won a significant number of seats in the European Parliament, it seems evident that a kenarchic, emancipatory feminism is needed that extends to all those who have been "transformed into symbolic and material scapegoats for the social decomposition effected by market deregulation that has a negative, degrading impact upon us all."[21] Kenarchic/feminist thinking must take into account that there are women and girls represented or affected in

19. Tyler, *Revolting Subjects*, 211.
20. Ibid., 3.
21. Ibid., 211.

all of the seven specific foci at the heart of Jesus' politics outlined by Haydon Mitchell in the Introduction.[22] Navigating the complexities of oppression, developing and drawing on insight with regard to agency and personal responsibility to build loving connections/relationships that run counter to sovereignty, must be part of our response to abject populations both within our national borders and beyond.

(ii) Thinking "intersectionally"

The academic Kimberlé Crenshaw has done important work in highlighting the complexity of oppression—and the extent to which black women can be "lost" in frameworks set up to combat racism and sexism because they are primarily focused on the problems of black men and white women. This "intersectionality" she identified[23] has become increasingly prominent in the context of digital feminism. As we will see, the potential of digital media for activism is being explored by women worldwide, although the focus of the British mainstream media remains largely on the strand that is dominated by white, predominantly middle-class feminists, particularly on issues of identity and representation, such as the number of women in the boardroom, or women on banknotes.[24]

Attempts by women of color to challenge white, middle-class women's dominance of the agenda have subsequently been criticized by a number of prominent white feminists who resist the need to include race in the gender debate, on the basis that it is potentially divisive. In the context of this debate a prominent blogger, Mikki Kendall, launched a hashtag called

22. See p. 11.

23. *1989 University of Chicago Legal Forum 1989 Demarginalizing the Intersection of Race and Sex: A Black Feminist Critique of Antidiscrimination Doctrine, Feminist Theory and Antiracist Politics.* N.p., n.d. Web. Accessed May 27, 2014.

24. Zoe Williams, "It's Boudicca v Bank of England in the Battle of the Banknotes." *The Guardian.* Guardian News and Media, July 6, 2013. Web. Accessed May 27, 2014.

#SolidarityIsForWhiteWomen that quickly went viral. Explaining the reason she started the hashtag, Kendall wrote: "It appeared that these feminists were, once again, dismissing women of color (WOC) in favor of a brand of solidarity that centers on the safety and comfort of white women."[25]

In a piece I wrote called "Five Rules For White Feminists,"[26] I argued that in order to engage with and contribute to the debate more constructively, it is essential that we embrace "white woman" as a political term. This will also help us move away from the assumption that our position is universal and develop a standpoint from which it is possible to divest ourselves of the hierarchical power of our identity. This is, of course, a difficult path to navigate, because it requires white women to embrace an identity of both victim of sovereignty and patriarchy and—perhaps less familiarly—as perpetrators of the same. But drawing on Jesus' self-emptying love gives us hope for a journey that frees us personally from sovereign power as we commit to building loving connections and relationships that subvert it.

Finding a way to build relationships with women of all races and classes that undermine imperial sovereignty seems particularly important at a time when the "discursive" offspring of feminism has, as Fraser suggests, "gone rogue."[27] A relational approach that seeks to respect "the other" and a historical awareness of how feminist ideas have been co-opted by sovereignty is needed "as we operate on a terrain that is also populated by [a movement for gender justice's] uncanny double."[28]

25. Mikki Kendall, "#SolidarityIsForWhiteWomen: Women of Color's Issue with Digital Feminism." *Theguardian.com*. Guardian News and Media, Aug. 14, 2013. Web. May 27, 2014.

26. Julie Tomlin, "Five Rules for White Feminists." Digital Women UK. N.p., Mar. 7, 2014. Web. Accessed May 27, 2014.

27. Fraser, *The Fortunes of Feminism,* 224.

28. Ibid., 225.

(iii) Women and war

Such an approach is particularly relevant in relation to what Nina Power describes as "one of the more profound and disturbing recent shifts in geopolitical discourse" – "the co-opting of the language of feminism" by those who previously would have opposed it.[29] The result, Power writes, is an imperialist feminism "that uses the language of liberal feminism (extending human rights, extending the vote) but the techniques of war."[30] As Faludi describes, in the lead up to the Afghanistan invasion, the plight of women in Afghanistan took on a new prominence. Burka-clad women became a staple of TV news as the then Secretary of State Colin Powell promised that "the rights of the women of Afghanistan will not be negotiable" and President George Bush signed the Afghan Women and Children Relief Act in December 2001.[31] Such a commitment was not followed through, however, and groups such as the Feminist Majority have charged the Bush administration with betraying their promises.[32] The perception that sympathy evoked by stories about women's oppression can be used to galvanize support for war was revealed in a cable, published by WikiLeaks, which said Afghan women could serve as "ideal messengers in humanizing the [International Security Assistance Force] role in combating the Taliban because of women's ability to speak personally and credibly about their experiences under the Taliban, their aspirations for the future, and their fears of a Taliban victory."[33] Awareness of the ways that, in an increasingly globalized world, stories about women's suffering can be used to strengthen support for imperial sovereignty, requires critical thinking if we are rather to engage with and contribute to an agenda that challenges economic subjection, dehumanization, and abjection.

29. Power, *One-dimensional Woman*, 11.

30. Ibid., 11.

31. Faludi, *The Terror Dream*, 40.

32. Ibid., 41.

33. Jeremy Scahill, "WikiLeaks and War Crimes." *The Nation*. N.p., n.d. Web. May 27, 2014.

DISRUPTING IMPERIAL NARRATIVES

What follows are examples of women's activism that challenge some entrenched attitudes that are an expression of sovereignty, and provide some pointers for further exploration of the shape a radical, personal politics of self-emptying love might take in this context.

The historic tendency of the West to demonize colonial peoples and their sexuality, for instance, could be seen in the British media's coverage of the rape and murder of a young woman in Delhi, who, along with her companion, was attacked by a gang on a bus in India's capital. There was little coverage of the nationwide protests condemning the attack that drew thousands of people, including young men, week after week. While I am not advocating that we ignore such events, we must also think critically about our response and the assumptions we make, and be careful to listen to what women on the ground are saying.[34]

When the wave of demonstrations and protests that were called the "Arab Spring" started in 2010, many British journalists seemed surprised that women took part in the protests. In reality, this is more to do with a particular blind spot with regard to women and protest: this is as true of women's struggles against land privatization in the sixteenth century as those staged at the beginning of the twenty-first century by Christian and Muslim Liberian women whose remarkable struggle for peace is captured in the film *Pray the Devil Back to Hell*—and the ongoing naked protests of the women of the Niger Delta against multinational oil companies. Because the media today focuses so rarely on stories that demonstrate women's agency, there is a dangerous tendency to treat stories about women's protests as a novelty.

Disrupting the dominant narrative of women around the world being in need of "saving" by the West, requires us also to be alert to the role played by NGOs that have "emerged everywhere to fill the space filled by shrinking states."[35] While acknowledging

---

34. Sunny Hundal, *What Indian Women Have Said on Delhi Gang-rape | Liberal Conspiracy*. Web. May 27, 2014.

35. Fraser, *The Fortunes of Feminism*, 221.

the good that many of them do, particularly supporting women and girls around the world, we must take heed of the criticism on the ground that they demonstrate imperial and colonial attitudes, skew agendas in the direction of funding nations, and depoliticize local grassroots movements. In the case of the #BringBackOur-Girls campaign, the plight of the kidnapped 200-plus girls in Nigeria attracted worldwide media attention as a result of a grassroots campaign, supported by African digital feminists. Although it is impossible to control such campaigns once they become global, disrupting imperial superiority in this context may mean finding ways of supporting and amplifying the voices of grassroots activists, while at the same time resisting efforts of western-based NGOs and campaigners to co-opt or "colonize" it.[36]

As well as exploring ways of engaging with women around the world which challenge the rescue narrative, we can also learn from the past and develop an awareness of how concern for their plight often fails to focus on systems of economic and social exploitation or acknowledge our national responsibility. For example, Dalit women in India are sometimes forced to work round the clock to meet orders for high street chains.[37] The collapse of a garment factory in Bangladesh in 2013 resulted in the death of more than 1000 people, many of them women. Despite initial concern about factory conditions, the rights of the women working in factories does not attract attention as a "women's issue" as cultural and sexual oppression does. Similarly, when a number of sexual assaults took place in Cairo's Tahrir Square in the midst of the protests in Egypt, the Western media reverted to traditional assumptions about the vulnerability of Egyptian women. Yet, economic practices that impact women's lives rarely come into focus, a fact summed up by a young activist Salma Said, who, asked by an audience member

36. Julie Tomlin, "How Do We #BringBackOurGirls?" *The Huffington Post UK*. Web. Accessed May 26, 2014.

37. Pauline Overeem, Martje Theuws, Marijn Peepercamp, and Gerard Oonk, *Maid in India: Young Dalit Women Continue to Suffer Exploitative Conditions in India's Garment Industry*. Rep. no. 3783. Centre for Research on Multinational Corporations (SOMO) and the India Committee of the Netherlands, Apr. 2012. Web. Accessed May 27, 2014.

at a talk in London what could be done to help Egyptian women, responded: "Stop your government selling weapons to the people who are shooting us."[38]

This final example exemplifies the direction that a kenarchic-inspired feminism should take: the Judaea Capta symbolizing woman's capacity to struggle, contextualized within the pursuit of a politics of peace that resists imperial sovereignty both individually and corporately and has in its sights the realization of the world Mary Cappe envisioned 350 years ago.

38. Tomlin, http://www.huffingtonpost.co.uk/julie-tomlin/arms-trade-women-the-arms-trade-is-a-femin_b_1672155.html.

3

The Gift of Woman

A Metaphor of Marginality

Sue Mitchell

IN HER WONDERFULLY DENSE overview of the historical development of feminism, Tomlin Arram has referenced key stories and developments; to this precise historical foreground I now add a metaphorical backwash of color, shape, and impression which informs my own journey to learn from the marginalized journey of womanhood.

LIMINALITY

If we take an interpretative direction from the creation metaphor,[1] as woman emerges alongside her male precursor, together they image the fullness of personhood. Her distinctive, as she comes from the dark, inside place rather than the overt, seen place, is

1. Gen 2:22–23; 5:1–2.

to dream dreams and gestate alternative possibilities. She enters into what is "before" her, which could be expected to be patriarchal, material, and organizational, while she is pre- (and equally comfortably post-) material, pre-logical (and equally comfortably post-secular); she is connective, intuitive, and, perhaps essentially, challenging to the status quo. Like Mary Cappe, woman is, symbolically, humanity attuned firstly to an inner voice, "the importance of the inner spirit or conscience," as Tomlin Arram has it, or which Viktor Frankl refers to as "the spiritual unconscious" or otherwise as the human conscience.[2]

If metaphorically woman represents the liminal space, she does so to signal its importance and to hold it open for humans to stand together where the need arises to question and challenge that which the conscience abhors, and confront dominance and injustice. The powerful in all generations must therefore determine the destruction of such challenging space, with woman often bearing the onslaught, sometimes in head-on opposition, but more usually and effectively by colonization. Over time the metaphor resonates less and less, as the liminal is incrementally absorbed into the dominant model. Remember Nina Power's acute observation in the previous chapter, and notice McKinney's examples of women's experience of "justice" in chapter 4.

Woman signaling the marginal space is wonderfully complemented by male recognition of and identification with this objectively moral position, as well as grievously by its denial by many good women, whose worldview and experience have been deeply affected by patriarchal and Christendom teaching of a compliant and submissive role to male authority. Nonetheless, though we now deal with human liminal experience of marginality in the light of global biopower's preening dominance, we focus here on the history of woman's struggle with power and powerlessness as essentially the most revelatory experience of that conflict between the sovereign and the liminal, subsequently intensified by other marginalization such as in women who are also black and poor. The struggle of the feminist movement itself, unfortunately to this

2. Frankl, *Man's Search for Ultimate Meaning*, Ch. 2 and Ch. 3, para 2.

point, does not quite succeed in this, though we should perhaps not be surprised about the implosion of the structural critique envisaged by the early feminists. The hegemonic assimilation process, which offers a measure of "multiplied sovereignty"[3] to as many identity interest groups as necessary to dull each to the needs of another, or even better to set them to compete with each other, has ever been the means to blunt the edge of the sharp threshing instrument of an awakened multitude.

OTHER

Metaphorically, the creation story has woman formed as distinct and other than man, necessitating collaborative reflection about what it might be to be human, and how that might be worked out in practice. The issue of how to act in and from the liminal space is a notoriously difficult one, simply because of the strength of the models in the "normal" or dominant space and its perpetual assimilation process. The theme of so many of the stories of women in the previous chapter, and those people speaking from other margins in the other contributions to this collection, is that the dominant behavior in the history of sovereignty is predatory, which holds its power by generating a mirrored response of victimhood in the marginalized. It feeds on competition and control, rather than collaboration, a distinction that Knox helpfully and practically explores in chapter 6 in the context of health provision. It is time to imagine creative responses, to avoid remaining in passive victimhood or, perhaps more significantly, reacting in violent or equally dominant behavior against the oppressor, even if intercessorily on behalf of others.

For instance, though the motif of Judaea Capta interpreted and celebrated Hannah Duston's bold struggle against captivity, the subsequent brutality of the retributive scalping of her captors might challenge the hearer.[4] If it does not challenge, it may be that

---

3. Mitchell, *Church, Gospel, and Empire*, 16–17.
4. See p. 32.

the predator instinct has become our only perceived alternative to victimhood. Certainly the media, blockbuster films, superhero narratives, and the democratic process only ever offer us the two behaviors to choose between. But as woman "was taken out of Man"[5] and since man has been born of woman,[6] we are mandated to recognize our shared identity in both responses, one as "both victim of sovereignty and patriarchy and—perhaps less familiarly—as perpetrators of the same"[7] and seek a different way.

TRANSCENDENCE

The creation metaphor is developed in the New Testament narrative as the discovery of a love able to transcend the divide between the self and "the other," and between the way things have been hitherto and the imagination of a different future. Paul references the need for a super-natural love when he likens the practice of the shared life of man and woman, those made differently though of the same nature, to the way Christ embraces humanity.[8] Studies in the psychology of love for "the other" have typically examined the motivation of what is gained by the lover, based in a worldview of evolutionary egoism. Only recently has research even considered that "valuing another individual's welfare" might be a possible alternative motivation which "awaits test."[9] Yet psychological and developmental studies are now also beginning to use the terminology of transcendence as something to be achieved beyond the biological and psychological drives associated with earlier research, as in Abraham Maslow's later hierarchy of needs model.[10] Today the word connotes different things in different contexts, but certainly denotes surpassing the "normal." A kenarchic approach

5. Gen 2:23.

6. 1 Cor 11:12.

7. See p. 38.

8. Eph 5:25.

9. Batson, Ahmed and Lishner, "Empathy and Altruism," 422.

10. See, for instance, Koltko-Rivera, *Rediscovering the Later Version of Maslow's Hierarchy of Needs*, 302–17.

recognizes the absolute necessity of, and access to, transcendent love to surpass individual self-interest in the light of the goal for "a new heaven and a new earth,"[11] in itself a vision and hope which transcends any human realism. As a final chapter, Scott therefore courageously reassesses the way in which even this hope has been assimilated by a dominant Christendom, and recontextualizes the challenging ethics of such an eschatological worldview.

It is not surprising to remember that formerly when those in the liminal space functioned in a way which did challenge the values of the status quo and which could be termed "transcendent," it often evoked the most violent response and against women, an accompanying vilification of morality and transcendence, in the accusation of witchcraft, which could be inferred from their "lack of deference."[12] A similar lack of deference to the power structures was evident in the stories of women drawn to the transcendent liminality of Jesus, and similar accusations of sexual looseness were made about them. Yet Jesus, on his journey to redeem humanity, recognized their gift and positioned himself to learn from and with them. So we now consider the backwashed outlines of the women that he so valued, who prefigured the feminist journey.

THE MOTHER

The revelation of the conception of a new humanity broke out in a song of understanding that this must redefine the social construction of a hierarchical system. It will scatter the proud, bring down "the rulers from their thrones," and exalt the humble. It will feed the hungry and displace the rich.[13] Learning at his mother's knee, Jesus was trained to question how things are and how they might be otherwise, and became adept at it in rabbinical school.[14] It is he

---

11. Rev 21:1.
12. See p. 33.
13. Luke 1:51–53.
14. Luke 2:46–47.

who was then surprised when his mother reverted to expecting him to follow social or familial rules.

Mike Love, whose heartfelt exploration of peacemaking is told in chapter 7, summed up this lesson, from Mary to Jesus and back again, as "disregarding the structures." They are, as we now generally accept in the twenty-first century, only social constructs, but seem to hold real power. Nonetheless, this power exists only as a "political imagination"[15] into which we all unthinkingly invest, until we do not. Mary sang of another way of being from that in which we have all been pre-consciously immersed, which rose from the spiritual level of moral awareness and choice. Jesus learned from the mother to see and choose differently from the social norms of the day.

The later interaction between Jesus and his mother at a family wedding then challenges our expectations of how both he and she "ought" to behave. "Woman, what does this have to do with me?"[16] is such a provoking question, unless perhaps we read it in the light of the intended collaboration between what is and what might be. What if Jesus, standing representatively in the dominant reality, truly asks what marginal sight might have to say differently?[17] Mary's answer is the voice of community instead of construct, expresses the felt shame in place of condemning it, and challenges excuses that will not embrace human need. Chastened by woman's gift, Jesus answers to this humanity and effects the change from outward discipline to inner community. He acts as if the water for the rites of purification, representing the society of control, were simply water; thus he "disregards" and empties it of its imagined substance. And he gives wine for the joy of uninhibited interaction, permissioning the messiness of human "imperfection," thus emptying the controlling myth of a falsely perfect humanity of its imagined substance too.

Evocative at so many levels, the contemporary experience of the Niger Delta women challenges us in a similar way. In a deep

15. Cavanaugh, *Theopolitical Imagination*, 1.

16. John 2:4 ESV.

17. Again, Love's chapter 7 is commended for a similar enquiry.

cultural ritual, the imagined substance of the shame of a woman's nakedness with the accusative connotations of her unclean sexuality was turned on its head. Here, for a woman to take off her clothes is a shocking demonstration to the watching men, reminding them that they come from this body and are fully identified with it. In profoundly powerful protest, women of the Niger Delta have stood naked in demonstrations against the giant oil companies and the devastating impact of oil spills on the land. The owners' heartlessness is shamed in its turn by the exposure of the dignified humanity to which they owe allegiance. It is a vivid metaphor for the way in which biopower has reduced everything it touches to "naked life";[18] the truly unashamed naked Life of these women empties out the imputed shame, and gives voice to the true interpersonal nature of unrighteousness.

THE ABJECT[19] ONE

In his interaction with the Canaanite woman[20] Jesus is further challenged, and we have to ask what this means. Kenarchy is the attempt to explore the poured-out-ness of Jesus the man, who, equal with God, emptied himself,[21] and Haydon Mitchell interrogates the substance of this profound attitude in the first chapter. It is crucial to our understanding both of Jesus' revelation of who God is and *therefore* of who persons, made in his image, are able to be. Richard Rohr[22] refers to the early church fathers' ease with the "divinization" of people, lost to us through the Western power narrative; it is an understanding to which we must return for humanity to be truly re-imaged. Jesus, of like nature with the transcendent God, embraces a life journey of relationship, love, and of true equality, and we see him in this encounter actually

18. Mitchell, *The Fall of the Church*, 62.
19. See ch. 2.
20. Matt 15:22–28.
21. Phil 2:7.
22. Rohr, *Falling Upward*.

change and develop. And in this we see both the full personality of the godhead (inevitably a trinity), as well as the divine nature of which we are also formed, as persons. "This goes to the heart of kenarchy . . . God surrenders any legitimate claim to sovereign power for the sake of love,"[23] not only when he becomes man, but always; the One God is always by nature Love, which can never dominate, but in relationship will always adapt and develop. As he re-walked the human journey in relational collaboration, God and the true human Self are revealed as of the same quality, a personhood which necessitates eschewing self-oriented power, in favor of mutual relationship.

So as he discipled his humanity to its divine potential, Jesus revealed the human and, indeed, transcendent struggle. It is the choice between the will to seemingly vulnerable love in the embrace of "the other," and every other temptation to the false or shadow humanity of Self-preservation in the will to power. And in this struggle we see him learn that unconsciously received mindsets resource the will to power. Unconscious, they are impossible to discern without being exposed by an "other," so inclusive approach towards those in the furthest margins is again revealed as our hope and salvation.

He falls silent in the face of a racially and culturally different woman who comes towards him crying out for help for her afflicted daughter. His male disciples are not silent. They tell him to send her away because her noisy intrusion is disturbing them. His own internal struggle is expressed, "I was sent only to the lost sheep of Israel." His deeply held belief, based in an inherited cultural experience of historical genocide and religious separation between Israelite and Canaanite peoples, is being challenged. She kneels and speaks from her heart. He struggles again with "It is not right to take the children's bread and throw it to the dogs." Neither seeking to justify her own rights or identity, nor correct his, she responds out of love for her daughter, "Even the dogs eat the crumbs . . ."[24] Her heart wisdom appeals to a common creation,

23. See p. 20.
24. Matt 15:21–28 NIV.

even with animal kind, and this inclusivity, this heartfelt emptying out of her own rights for the sake of reaching this healing, finds a transcendent resonance in Jesus who joins her in her choice of being lovingly given to another. In this place, the future is healed.

The ability to see from a different perspective is always easier if we can borrow an Other's eyes. It is the failure to choose to do so which Tomlin Arram points to concerning the new perspectives emerging from Arab, African, and Indian political protests and the grassroots movements that are engaging so effectively in today's struggles for change, often led by "unseen" women. A kenarchic approach to epistemology encourages a "standpoint" position, which Haydon Mitchell cites from Ward's work, and which draws "on the work of Marxist and feminist thinkers, [and] emphasizes the way in which the emergence of a standpoint is concerned with minority perspectives."[25] Ward particularly quotes feminist theologians Sandra Harding and Nancy Hartstock,[26] who together with others "develop an epistemology with respect to seeing things from the perspective of women's lives." Jesus certainly took this journey towards understanding truth gleaned from the margins, following the leadership of such excluded women.

THE EXTRAVAGANT[27] ONE

Towards the end of his journey, Jesus is supported in his demanding final steps by the welcome at Bethany, and the prophetic wastage of Mary's precious ointment.[28] Here indeed we see a prefiguring of Faludi's insight that woman's dramatic, prophetic intelligence is so often recast as "hysterical . . . requiring male salvation,"[29] which Judas's reaction embodies. But Mary is also towards the end of her own learning journey to be one comfortable with the margins. She

25. Mitchell, *Church, Gospel, and Empire*, 208.

26. Harding, *Whose Science? Whose Knowledge?* and Hartstock, *The Feminist Standpoint Revisited and Other Essays,* cited in Ward, 73.

27. "Extravagant" from the Latin root "to wander outside and beyond."

28. John 12:1–8.

29. See Tomlin Arram, 33.

may have learnt from and copied the gesture of "the woman of the city" in Simon's house[30] in the earlier account of anointing, or perhaps been her (it appears to be a different event, though might allow for Mary being the actor in both[31]). Both as the woman there, and later as Mary took part in education from which woman was normally excluded,[32] she has learnt to disregard both the accusative judgments of the dominant reality and the criticism of others on the margins angry at the challenge to their own victimhood. Jesus ratifies marginal, affective understanding as a vital contribution to redeemed human perception in "Mary has chosen what is better,"[33] and by his own narrative response about love and forgiveness to the Pharisee's heartless challenge.[34] Finally, today, the control of so-called "rationality," the "scientific method," and the matheses of belief systems which define exclusivity are beginning to give way to enquiry, imagination, and affective influence such as transcendent hope, faith, and a confidence that can embrace difference. It has been the grace from the margins of people, often of womankind, embracing rejection as a redemptive gift and transcending their prescribed sense of self which has contributed to this moment of possibility.

Nonetheless, there remains the dominant language, the permanent weight of crushing economic control that continually reinforces marginalization and cynically undermines hope by its sheer universality. The empire of global capital is the means and end of the biopower which boundaries every moment of our lives, as Haydon Mitchell spells out in the Introduction. Mary marvelously resisted this proscription of what she had and was. Judas valued her perfume economically; she perceived the "'emotional and spiritual content' present in [it as] a gift,"[35] and "wandering

---

30. Luke 7:37ff.

31. See John 11:1 which could refer either retrospectively to this earlier account, or forward to the following chapter.

32. Luke 10:39.

33. Luke 10:42 NIV.

34. Luke 7:39ff.

35. See p. 66.

outside or beyond" the economic model of exchange, emptied its prophetic substance into an alternative value system. As Rusk quotes enticingly in his radical imagination of such a different system in chapter 5, "the choice to give graciously is both hopeful and anti-cynical. It is an attempt to start something new."[36]

The voices and strategies from the margins call us passionately and creatively to this hopeful newness.

36. See p. 72.

4

Criminal Justice on the Margins

Victims, Perpetrators, and Restorative Relationships

Peter McKinney

INTRODUCTION

Kenarchy has a clear direction, like the life of Jesus, towards those marginalized and on the wrong side of harsh dividing lines of class, wealth, gender, and guilt—issues that cut to the heart of human compassion and love. This "direction" of kenarchy is for me both a foundation for understanding what it means to live like Jesus, and at the same time a pivot on which very real decisions can be made in the face of human suffering and trauma. Decisions to offer food, comfort, shelter, advice, compassion; decisions to speak up for those who can't, to speak truth in the face of a system that doesn't question systemic injustice. These are decisions rooted in kenarchy, and they are 100 percent political—they seek an alternative future to the status quo.

This chapter is my attempt to reflect on kenarchy out of my experience working with many people who could be described as marginalized and socially excluded in Ireland, North and South, over the last ten years. This experience has brought me into contact with those suffering addiction, imprisonment, homelessness, family breakdown, and multiple levels of disempowerment, compounded by a distinct lack of the family and social supports that usually help most of us get through tough times. Such marginalization is of course invented, as the margins are only such in relation to a "center." Thus my reflection is tinged with the very real understanding of my (and our) tacit complicity in the "system" that underpins the center and therefore the "margins." It is here that I start, on the margins and amongst those who are usually lumped together in our social narrative as non-individuals—the homeless, addicts, victims, perpetrators, too often castigated as down and outs, immoral, mad, powerless. This is the language of the margins, but if "we" as society have structured it this way, surely then we can change it. For me it is here on the center-margin that the dynamic of kenarchy comes into play.

KENARCHY AND CRIMINAL JUSTICE

What does this mean for us day to day? The above statement challenging the current center/margin injustice calls for nothing less than kenarchic revolution that places the marginalized as the focus for how we shape society, a corrective rebalancing of priorities.

I am all too aware that what I have said still remains theoretical. I want to draw from my own experience in order to point in a direction of where this may be leading. Part of my previous career touched on the criminal justice system, and perhaps the best example I can offer of how transformation can, and should, occur is reflected in how our society deals with the ideas of justice and criminality, first generally and then specifically in the context of women offenders.

What has fascinated me about working with offenders has been the realization, challenging my own stereotypes, that they too are "victims" as well as "perpetrators." This issue of the victim/perpetrator, and in particular how it is experienced by women, has been for me the most recent "revealing" of what lies beneath our commonly held, and commonly agreed, practice of "justice," and it is a sphere within which I believe there is a huge opportunity for real alternative practice.

(i) Ideas of justice

The majority of models of justice we know today are based on a clear principle of crime and punishment. Prevalent in these models is an understanding that retribution is "OK" when you have been wronged. So, if someone steals from me, defrauds me, or attacks me, they should be caught and punished with a sentence that "reflects the severity of the crime." To many this is not only normal, but surely just and right, as well as a deterrent to those who would abuse others in this way. In many ways I wholeheartedly agree, and I want to state clearly that I am not belittling the impact of a crime, both materially and personally, nor the good I have seen worked through our broken system. However, to get at the depths of the transformative love of Jesus and what living kenarchically might mean, we must ask difficult questions taking us to the edge of what we find comfortable, in fact beyond it. And so by questioning the above logic, held to be sound, another reading of the process involved can emerge.

Firstly, it is limited in scope, in that it focuses on the crime in question, taking limited account of context. Secondly, it is "crime-centered" and not either victim- or perpetrator-centered. Thirdly, little consideration is given as to whether the end result—punishment—actually changes behavior or benefits society. Instead, it is taken as implicitly the right route. I would suggest that if we truly want the outcomes we desire from our criminal

justice system—consequences for crime, victim satisfaction, reha-
bilitation and reduced offending, a safer society—the whole idea of
retribution in our justice system needs questioning at every level.

(ii) The victim

The victim is often disempowered in our society. Not long ago I
was told the following story by a friend in law enforcement, which
provides us with several pointers as to how "justice" can look different, and be worked out in a different, more relational way. A
man reported to the police that money had been stolen from his
bank account. Initial police enquiries quickly identified that the
suspect was his housekeeper, who had worked for him for years,
and the housekeeper was duly spoken to by the police. The man,
however, requested that he be given the opportunity to talk to
her. He sat with her, asked her directly what had happened, and
gained a full confession and explanation of the reasons why she
had committed the crime. He then talked to the officers involved,
explaining that he did not want to make a formal complaint or
comply with an investigation or seek the funds returned. While
the woman would not work for him again as she had broken trust,
having confronted her and heard her reasons for her actions, he
had decided he did not want the matter pursued.

In my friend's view, in this instance, even though in terms of
police statistics the crime wasn't "solved," justice had been served.
Why? The victim had been able to process his feelings of disappointment and gain understanding of what had happened and
why, and the perpetrator had been able to confess, say sorry, and
explain her side of the story. A two-sided resolution of the crime
had taken place that in many ways excluded the criminal justice
system, and for both parties a line had been drawn under it. Whilst
the woman lost her job, she did not go to prison. Whilst the victim did not see criminal punishment enacted, he was satisfied that
the issue had been resolved and that he had received redress. This
outcome did several things. Both parties left "freer," with resolution in questions answered and the issue confronted. The officers

involved had less paperwork to go through, society did not have to fund a potential legal process or indeed a custodial sentence, and, importantly, the housekeeper, who was in tears during the whole process, left in no doubt that she had both suffered consequences and been shown mercy and granted a chance to change.

This anecdote reflects some of the principles of growing restorative justice practices and approaches around the world today,[1] that are very different to what we have known in the past, where everyone has the potential to be a winner, and the opportunity to change.

The victim holds a deeper power than any judge—the power to forgive. This is what the story of Jesus models: having the power to hold many in "judgment" but rather taking an alternative choice, opening up an all-encompassing flow of love, forgiveness, restoration, and life. One reading of Jesus is that he emptied out the retributive and violent system he lived in, journeying through the capital punishment it imposed, but in the mystery of resurrection transforming it, and exposing it for what it is, a consequence of the dysfunction of social relationships, devoid of love and hope. Jesus emptied out our dysfunctional and cyclical victim and perpetrator violence.[2] We are both complicit and trapped in the cycle. An alternative future is needed, and we must not rob victims of the opportunity to forgive and seed transformation.

(iii) Punishment fits the crime

Without doubt there is a hierarchy of crime. It is more impacting on me if I have my jaw broken in an assault than if I have my watch stolen. This is recognized. What is also recognized in our current system is the idea that there are sometimes reasons for a crime and these should be taken into account. I argue that an understanding

1. For case studies, service maps, and research of restorative justice practices (UK and Ireland) see the Restorative Justice Council (www.restorativejustice.org.uk) and from a community perspective see Community Restorative Justice Ireland (www.crji.ie).

2. Alison, *The Joy of Being Wrong*.

of the background behind the crime should be a shaping factor for the system itself, not an "extra" during sentencing. Recent exploration in the criminology of "social harm"[3] offers a more holistic perspective on these issues, and many organizations and reform groups have been calling for the widespread adoption of alternatives to prison for those who commit crime but who are, for example, addicted to drugs or are being given custodial sentences for petty crimes and non-payment of fines.[4] Our prisons are filled with such people, often in need of therapeutic care or other supports rather than prison. Where alternatives to custody have been trialed in the UK, they have been found to be both cheaper and more effective in reducing re-offending.[5] In Northern Ireland, with its chequered history, there are many and varied restorative justice projects that are working in local communities in a post-conflict society, offering alternative forms of reconciliation and local and community-based responses to crime.[6] An additional benefit of these projects is that they also have an aspect of community ownership, a key point for areas in Northern Ireland where people hold a historical mistrust of the police. The fight for the future is still being fought in Northern Ireland (we call it "Dealing with the Past") literally in terms of retribution and restoration, with victims' groups speaking up for those they feel have not had justice, and with others calling the "past the past" and seeking to draw a line. My point here is not on one side or the other—there is enough of victim and perpetrator to go around if you look hard

3. Hillyard and Tombs, "From 'Crime' to Social Harm," 9–25.

4. IPRT Position Paper 10: Women in the Criminal Justice System – Towards a non-custodial approach (2013). Available from http://www.iprt. ie/files/IPRT_Position_Paper_on_Women_in_the_Criminal_Justice_System.pdf.

5. For an evaluation of one of the only alternatives to custody services in the UK see this research in the 218 Project in Glasgow: http://www.turning-pointscotland.com/wp-content/uploads/2011/03/218-evaluation.pdf .

6. A good overview of services was conducted in the Queen's University Mapping Exercise in conjunction with the Restorative Justice Forum NI. http://www.quakerservice.com/Mapping-Report-Restorative-Practices-in-Northern-Ireland-Nov-2010.pdf.

enough or go back far enough—the point is that in this fissure, in the tug of war between the two "pulls" into one or the other, lies space for relationship that provokes a process. While change is happening, it is not without strong challenge, and more of the space we have at this moment needs to be filled with kenarchic restorative relationships, not retributive cyclical dysfunction. For our conversation in this chapter, the above examples point to a complication of "crime and punishment" as a system, and to an infinitely varied and life-giving opportunity to exit this cycle and for restorative work to occur, with potential to free both the victim and the perpetrator and, in so doing, free us all.

WOMEN AND CRIMINAL JUSTICE

To dig just a bit deeper on this issue, looking at the highly marginalized experience of women offenders offers us an opportunity to explore ideas of exclusion and restoration, and show succinctly the underlying structures that shape much of our society's response to crime.

The first thing to highlight is that there is a "double guilt" involved. Society has certain expectations of female behavior, and crime and violence are on the other end of the spectrum. Women committing crime is thus more "against nature" than that committed by men. This is historical, layered, and complex, but it is clear that we are (still) emerging from dominant patriarchy in the West. I am unashamedly a feminist for this very reason. In the news every week the issue of patriarchy and women is bubbling to the surface like never before: from the plight of women under Taliban rule in Afghanistan to the controversy of ordaining a woman bishop in the Church of England, these issues are varied, prevalent, and are increasing in frequency and gravity. I say this to point to the fact that still there is a "male center" and a "female margin" at work. For women at the receiving end of criminal justice, add to this marginalization the double guilt of criminality, and we see the context in which many women find themselves. A third level of systemic marginalization at work is wider than the individual and is about children. As women, in the majority of families, provide the primary care for children and a large proportion of the women who are imprisoned are single parents, the impact on those children (and on the women) during imprisonment is immeasurable.[7] This impacts the very fabric of society. An all-too-common theme in conversations with colleagues who work in this sector is the constant marvel at the intergenerational and repetitive nature of these issues.[8]

Having been privileged to spend time with many women experiencing such issues I have seen first-hand the above marginalization at work—the stereotyping and shame, the sheer lack of gender specific services and approaches within the system, and, perhaps most provokingly, the impact on children and the mother-child relationship. I have also seen how innovative approaches can work, and how they are so needed—within prison, during the court process, and after prison during re-integration. A kenarchic revolution that centers the margins for this group in our society could transform the above scenario.

Firstly, putting children first means not punishing them for others' wrongs. The needs of the child should without doubt outweigh much of what we hold to be foundational to "justice," and provide a whole new window through which to judge and indeed reconfigure our current pathways within criminal justice. Secondly, the specific needs of women should be a shaping factor for criminal justice responses. For example, as the types of crime committed by women are statistically mostly non-violent,[9] alternative

7. I use "immeasurable" advisedly and to emphasize the depth of human impact, especially on young children. This issue and that of generational impact of social interventions are key areas for research in trying to quantify impact, and also analyze cost-benefit more accurately. Whilst welcome, I also argue that this will never touch the depths of negative impact that can be avoided by positive alternative pathways.

8. For further reading on these issues from an Irish perspective (but pointing to international trends and research) see Quinlan, *Inside,* and the publications and briefing papers of the Irish Penal Reform Trust, especially "Picking Up the Pieces" and "Women in the Criminal Justice System" available at www.iprt.ie.

9. In Ireland in 2012 out of 2,071 women committals under sentence, 1,687

disposals and pathways avoiding custody should be used for a higher proportion of women offenders,[10] offering a wider variety of specific services addressing drug misuse, parenting capacity and child relationships, sexual health, and emotional and mental wellbeing. Lastly, a kenarchic approach that centers the margin is a corrective to patriarchy and the overarching narratives that marginalize women. This is not to say that feminism in itself is an end, but rather that maleness in itself needs to be cleansed from patriarchy. For women offenders, it challenges the shame of the double guilt and addresses the needs of women and children in a more holistic way with choices available to better address crime and support families.

SOWING GOOD SEED

I use the idea of a seedbed to describe the potential that the ideas of kenarchy have when coupled with those who are practicing peace-making across our societies. As well as a kenarchist I am an amateur gardener and wannabe prize pumpkin producer. I have just finished my internal sowing for this season, starting the process of raising seedlings in a protected and enriched environment, ready to transition them to larger pots and finally to their growing and fruiting positions. This for me is like kenarchy: dynamic life-filled ideas that, with stimulation, connection, roots, and timely exposure, can grow and produce huge impact and life. What I have raised in this chapter has, I hope, pointed to what might be considered some kenarchic seeds of change of a different way of living and doing our social relationships in criminal justice, how we handle the victim/perpetrator dilemma, and how we treat marginalized women and children. I am more convinced than ever that our society and relationships are looking for transformed and better ways of doing life, and it's time to make the connection. As

---

were for non-payment of fines (IPRT, "Picking Up the Pieces", p. 4).

10. Community service, for example, in Ireland at least, most often provides male-centered roles, and needs to be augmented by placements that encourage engagement and enables a viable non-custody pathway for women offenders.

such I do call for a kenarchic revolution where you are and in what you touch for a social and community rebalancing of priorities, knowing that only those who grab hold of a different future and don't let go will destabilize the status quo and bring life, a bit like what Jesus modeled.

5

The Politics of Gift

Stephen Rusk

KENARCHY, AS ARTICULATED IN this volume, is all about pouring out oneself as a gift for "the other," whoever that "other" may be. In sharp contrast to the world in which we live, which tends to be geared towards economy, appropriation, and profit, kenarchy deals in gift. Gift-giving—and receiving—is something that we all intuitively understand and, in most cases, enjoy at the interpersonal level to various degrees. Yet, the kenarchic imperative to live in a gift-oriented way is not restricted to the interpersonal. Indeed, it is deeply challenging to the political, economic, and social world around us. There is no mistaking it, living a gift-oriented life in a "take"-oriented world is swimming against the current. It is a political act of resistance built on belief in the endless possibility of love, community, and forgiveness. Such a manifesto is, then, also somewhat personally challenging, provoking as it does dilemmas about how to give, how much, and to what end. In the course of this short chapter I will draw out some of the main issues and implications of a gift-oriented politics.

GIFT, ECONOMY, AND RELATIONSHIP

Gift and economy are distinctly different. Most transactions in life are about balancing out payments and receipts: for everything given, something else is received. This equilibrium is what we call economy or exchange, in which nothing is given for free. In pure economy no one gains and no one loses in a transaction. Both parties remain in net terms as they were, having lost and gained in equal value.[1] A gift, however, deviates from this arrangement. With gifts, things are given without being sought and, ideally, without expectation of return. As John Caputo puts it, "there have to be things we do for the sheer love of them, things that are given to us to which we in turn give ourselves, where we break the chain of means-and-ends."[2] This is what gifts are about. My friend buys me lunch because he wants to and I get to benefit without recompensing him. What could be a more normal gesture of kindness and relationship? Except, as we all know, it's not quite so simple because there is not the closure that we usually expect with exchange. Things are left hanging. I am grateful for my friend's gesture but I also feel I want to do something in return. I have benefitted and I don't want this to be a one-way experience so I start thinking of ways I can extend a gift to my friend.

In this way, gifts disturb the social and economic balance between us. They are much more unruly and less predictable than economy. They are also inherently relational. In an economy, you can transact with anyone, regardless of whether you know them, with "no strings attached." The nature of the relationship need only be contractual and transitory. It is not necessary to scratch the surface or consider "the other's" welfare. Gifts, by contrast, are much more involved, creating bonds or obligations that last longer than the act of giving. In the sanitized world of economy, both parties can remain strangers to each other and certainly do not risk anything of themselves when they make a transaction. Gifts afford no

---

1. This is quite different from a capitalist market economy in which something additional is usually extracted by one party from the other as a profit.

2. Caputo, *What Would Jesus Deconstruct?*, 69.

such safety, even when given anonymously. Gift-giving anticipates some kind of ongoing relationship with "the other" and involves the risk that what one gives may or may not hit the intended mark. Gifts are thus of the order of faith while economy is about the mitigation of obligation or fear.

It is interesting what happens when we take gift and relationship out of the equation. Kester Brewin, drawing on Michael Sandel's 2009 Reith Lectures, tells how a nursery in Israel introduced a policy of fining parents for picking their children up late. Imagine their surprise when parents started turning up later than ever! As Brewin puts it, "the introduction of money removed any relational or empathetic obligation the parents may have felt to get to the nursery on time."[3] By contrast, in a gift environment we tend to give things greater value. A coffee shop has recently opened in my city where there are no prices for the food and drinks. There is no till and no suggested values for the services provided. Patrons are simply asked to make a donation before they leave. While this may seem a rather high-risk business strategy, it turns out that on average the coffee shop's customers are giving more than they could expect to pay in similar commercial coffee shops in the city.

What underlies these examples is the fact that gift involves "a relationship of recognition between giver and receiver"; economies do not.[4] Gifts are what scholars have referred to as a "total social phenomenon." They involve encountering our neighbor, the stranger, "the other." Economies avoid such awkwardness, invasion, and humanity, preferring instead the legalistic safety of balanced exchange. They shed the "emotional and spiritual content" present in a gift.[5] Certainly, there are times when this is preferable and I would hazard that few of us feel able to have meaningful relationship with every person we encounter. Yet, to the extent that we seek love, community, and peace, these things inevitably require the risk of a gift. This is why for the French philosopher Jacques

3. Brewin, *Other*, 200.

4. Kearney interviewed in "The Hermeneutics of the Gift: A Dialogue," in Stevenson, *Gift and Economy*, 79.

5. Hyde, *The Gift*, 88.

Derrida, gift is "the first mover of the circle."[6] What loving relationship ever began without gift? What vibrant community ever functioned on the basis of exchange alone, where people only did the minimum necessary to get something equal in return, where no one ever took the risk of giving something new to others? Fundamentally, the choice to give is a choice to prioritize community—in Levinas' terms to be "responsible for the Other."[7] As Haydon Mitchell has outlined already in this volume, "love begins with giving and receiving in mutual relationship and grows into a resource that can be shared."[8]

GIFT COMMUNITY

In his recent, popular book *Sacred Economics: Money, Gift and Society in the Age of Transition*, Charles Eisenstein laments the loss of community in the contemporary Western world. He rightly identifies that while "community is woven from gifts," our prevailing culture prioritizes individual independence through a system in which we are encouraged to behave as though we "do not need each other."[9] This atomization is, of course, rooted in the Western Enlightenment myth of the self-sufficient individual and allied to the concept of private property, an idea to which I will return shortly.

Kenarchy, however, proposes a radical and probably unfashionable alternative path in which we choose to love our neighbors, where we recognize our inter-dependency with others, particularly including those who are not like us. It is of course a positive thing to offer gifts and hospitality to those we already love, and doing so is an important part of sustaining and enriching community. Yet kenarchy goes further than simply securing the welfare of the community. In fact, it is prepared to take some risks. It takes issue with exclusionary social boundaries, no matter how valid or well

6. Derrida, *Given Time*, 30–31.
7. Levinas and Kearney, "Dialogue with Emmanuel Levinas."
8. See p. 12.
9. Eisenstein, *Sacred Economics*, 420–21.

intentioned they may seem. It advocates, like the Good Samaritan, crossing psychological and social barriers to prioritize "the other": "When you give a luncheon or a dinner, do not invite your friends or your brothers or your relatives or rich neighbors, otherwise they may also invite you in return and that will be your repayment. But when you give a reception, invite the poor, the crippled, the lame, the blind, and you will be blessed, since they do not have the means to repay you . . ."[10] The point here is that the gift carrying the greatest potential to change everyone involved is the one which crosses psycho-social boundaries, which does not worry about balance or fairness, and which multiplies loving connections beyond the current economy of relationship without expectation of return. This way lies the end of exclusivity and the fullness of St Paul's socio-political vision, in which "there is neither Jew nor Greek, . . . slave nor free man, . . . male nor female."[11] The alternative, as we have seen, is economy which does not share this trajectory but rather leaves the boundaries and the people involved more or less exactly as they were. Indeed, a more expropriative economy will often multiply those boundaries. Only gift-giving breaks the circle, to the cost of the one who gives.

POWER AND ECONOMY

Economies are inevitably and devastatingly subject to power and control. When this happens economies become vehicles for appropriation, profit, and usury. They are more about exploitation than exchange so that the powerful benefit at the expense of the others. Instead of equilibrium, some gain while others lose; some become rich while others become poor. If gift is about promoting the intrinsic value of relationship and community, these expropriative economies are about devaluing humanity, turning people into atomized commodities whose "surplus value" can be extracted. These economies are "the very antithesis of gift, for instead of

10. Luke 14:12–14.
11. Gal 3:28; cf. Col 3:11 and Eph 2:19.

giving to others when one has more than one needs, usury seeks to use the power of ownership to gain even more—to take from others rather than to give."[12] This is the harsh reality of the prevailing modern economy (built as it is on the prioritization of property over humanity) and the injustice that Karl Marx perceived at the core of capitalism.[13]

It is important to recognize at this point that even so-called "gifts" between individuals and groups can be used to manipulate or control others through the creation of indebtedness as part of an exploitative or self-aggrandizing agenda. Most of us have had experiences where gifts came with strings attached, where the cynical adage that there is "no such thing as a free lunch" appeared to hold truth. The giving of a gift or the offering of hospitality was in fact a power-play. It was designed to remind "recipients" and observers that the "giver" held the real power and hierarchical status. It might even have been an attempt to embarrass or demean. The truth is there was no gift at all, only the opposite.

The centrality accorded to ownership in the contemporary world derives from the way property and individualism have been fused in the foundations of the modern world since the Enlightenment. And it is clear to see how this happened. If, like Hobbes, you assume that human nature is ultimately selfish and that people are destined to war with each other,[14] it follows that you must be materially independent in order to be sure that you will be able to eat, have shelter, and so on. Then, if you take Locke's view that power comes from having property, indeed that property is what gives you the "power to act" in society,[15] then the accumulation of "stuff" is none other than the way to become free and to have the power to change your circumstances. This is how Rousseau could claim that property was "the most sacred of all the rights of citizens, and

12. Eisenstein, *Sacred Economics*, 94.

13. Marx and Engels, *The Communist Manifesto*.

14. Hobbes, *Leviathan*.

15. Balibar, "Possessive Individualism reversed," 302. See also Locke, "Second Discourse."

more important in some respects than freedom itself."[16] Inevitably, this perspective simply institutionalizes Hobbes' pessimism, forcing people to seek to out-do one another in order to have power and get on in life. The issue is not property itself but accumulating it beyond one's needs in order to have power over others. This approach is endemic in the prevailing contemporary system but it is not the only way of doing things.

MAKE IT A GIFT INSTEAD

Kenarchy's response to these kinds of power-play is nothing short of radical, whether at the level of society/economy or at the level of inter-personal encounters in everyday life. Indeed, the kenarchic manifesto set out in the Sermon on the Mount makes for quite uncomfortable reading, especially for the contemporary West. Through its counter-intuitive proposals, the Sermon puts gift-giving at the heart of kenarchic non-violent resistance:

> "You have heard that it was said, 'An eye for an eye, and a tooth for a tooth.' But I say to you, do not resist an evil person; but whoever slaps you on your right cheek, turn the other to him also. If anyone wants to sue you and take your shirt, let him have your coat also. Whoever forces you to go one mile, go with him two. Give to him who asks of you, and do not turn away from him who wants to borrow from you."[17]

This is kenarchy's response to the dominant expropriative systems: when something is taken from you, make it a gift instead. In fact, to the extent that you can do it graciously, give more than is demanded. This is radical stuff. But how can a gift given in love compete with the powers when the objective of boundary-breaking relationship and community is not shared? Surely the giving of gifts in this context will simply result in personal loss as the powerful

---

16. Rousseau, "Discourse on Political Economy (first version of the Social Contract)," 23.

17. Matt 5:38–42.

pursue their own ends by exploiting others' means? While it may be possible to build pockets of gift-oriented community, what part can gifts play in relation to the powerful? Such questions perhaps indicate why political philosophy has made only furtive attempts to explore a politics of love or gift. It is somewhat easier to conceive of self-interested politics, in which one fights one's corner, than it is the politics of gift.

Ultimately, however, kenarchy is not about competing with expropriative economies or individuals but rather proposes disregarding their power. Rather than accepting boundaries being drawn along the lines of power and the production of victimhood, kenarchy proposes what C. S. Lewis so famously animated in *The Lion, the Witch and the Wardrobe,* that there is a deeper magic more powerful than expropriation or even benign exchange.[18] Kenarchy proposes that this deeper magic is self-giving love or what Haydon Mitchell has termed "the giving of oneself within the gift of God's egalitarian grace to the farthest reach of the other's position, at the utter risk of one's own life."[19] This is no easy path and the problem for political philosophy is that this "infinite ethical demand"[20] cannot readily be translated into a practicable system or even a program of resistance. Indeed, this is also why the politics of gift is at least as problematic for religion (which seems so often in search of a system or program of devotion or confession).

To practice the politics of gift means for an individual, a community, or a people to risk their life or identity in one way or another. But the risk of a kenarchic gift, while profoundly revolutionary (no matter how small), is not cavalier or quixotic. It is not motivated by the heaping of coals on one's enemy's head or the desperate logic of the suicide bomber.[21] It is a huge, open invitation to be part of an alternative economy, a different social order moved by love, recognition, and relationship. The choice to

18. See Lewis, *The Lion, the Witch and the Wardrobe.*
19. Mitchell, *The Fall of the Church,* 102.
20. See Critchley, *The Faith of the Faithless.*
21. Cf. Rom 12:19–21; Prov 25:21–22.

give graciously is both hopeful and anti-cynical. It is an attempt to start something new.

TOWARDS A GIFT ECONOMY

I have consciously avoided in this chapter setting out any prescriptions for a "gift economy." To do so would undermine my point. Unlike economy, gifts do not have any equilibrium or predictability. There is no program or schema. For sure, the politics of gift has potentially major implications for economics, geopolitics, and the systems at work in our world. It will be important for these to be fully explored. But gift always begins with a very human, even visceral, choice to start a ball rolling. Gift flows from a desire for relationship and being present for "the other." Gifts are always in some way creative, whether through their inspiration, timing, the choice of what is given, or the message that they carry. There is no ten-step plan for setting up a gift economy and thereby transforming the world. That would be both ludicrous and patronizing. However, gifts beget gifts and, in doing so, they build relationship and create community. They are contagious and potentially viral, carrying the potential to challenge and expose expropriative systems. They don't have to be gifts of monetary value but they may cost you time, your reputation, or your mindset.

"Freely you received, freely give."[22]

---

22. Matt 10:8.

6

Kenarchy and Healthcare

Andy Knox

IN 2011 THE LATE Tony Benn did a piece for Channel 4 on the radical politics of Jesus. In talking about the world and how we interact with it, he said: "The most important thing of all is the teachings of Jesus in how we should treat each other . . . Social Justice is everything in politics. How I see my fellow men and women is absolutely crucial in interpreting the responsibilities I feel Jesus has imposed on me."[1] For me, this pinpoints a key issue that I have tried to address in my work in healthcare, which at its heart is about interaction with people and the way that people are treated matters at the most fundamental level.

The Health Service has become increasingly politicized. Elections are won and lost on promises made about the provision of healthcare. The UK has had a National Health Service (NHS) since 1948, but the current debate about the role of the state as funder of providers from the private sector, has raised concerns that the

1. T. Benn, *Tony Benn on Jesus*, 4thought.tv, July 2011,https://www.youtube.com/watch?v=d8qC8KKdkeU.

writing could be on the wall for universal healthcare that is independent of the ability to pay.

The NHS in the UK is a truly remarkable system that strives to provide excellent care for patients no matter what their socio-economic background. It is staffed by highly qualified people who desire to see people cared for with excellence and compassion.

However, with the introduction of market principles, there has been a shift away from a focus on service, towards commodification. With the introduction of the concept of healthcare as a source of profit, care often becomes secondary. A target-driven culture is allowing patients to be treated like numbers or entities. Although such targets are intended to "drive up standards" and "improve patient care," there are many examples where "payment by results" subtracts from patient-centered care.[2] It has become commonplace to hear of people referred to as "diabetics" or "asthmatics," for instance, which changes the focus from their being a person, with a name, who has diabetes or asthma.

In setting out some of the changes that are currently taking place in the health service, I hope to identify the potential of a kenarchic approach and the kind of actions it might lead to, particularly for those who work in this sphere.

SUBVERSION AND SUBMISSION

Working within the system provides many opportunities to subvert its dehumanizing effects, while choosing also to submit back into it in a way that has been referred to as a rhythm of life.

(i) Simple acts of love

Demonstrating servanthood, humility, forgiveness, or "going the extra mile" can in and of themselves be a challenge to the

2. C. Dowler, *Updated: NHS England and Monitor plan major reform of payment by results* (HSJ/Corporate, 2013), http://www.hsj.co.uk/news/finance/updated-nhs-england-and-monitor-plan-major-reform-of-payment-by-results/5058575.article#.UoRi9l7t1Fw.

dehumanizing effects of the system. The 95-year-old husband of a woman who has dementia and is doubly incontinent, told me, when I helped to move his wife from one chair to another and assisted with her hygiene, that her carers only seemed to "work to rule" and said such tasks were not in their "remit." I suppose they weren't in my official remit either. Guidelines, however, are not an excuse not to respond with humanity or love. I have frequently heard healthcare professionals say, "That's not my job," but that attitude has resulted in too many patients having been left unfed or with their bed unchanged for hours.

There are a number of problems to which these uncaring attitudes and lack of basic care point, including a practical one of understaffing, but also something deeper regarding the human ego and a selfishness which often pervades. These are tendencies that we must challenge in ourselves, by choosing to demonstrate love and servanthood.

(ii) Reconfiguring power

In my day-to-day life, I've tried to reflect this in the choices I make: for example, by cleaning up the mud from the surgery floor when a patient has trampled it through the building and the cleaner is off sick, and asking all my patients to call me Andy, instead of Dr Knox—although I never enforce this! These simple actions, I hope, help make it clear to them that knowledge is relational and, with me in the role of adviser rather than guru, we can share our knowledge with one another and come to a joint place of understanding and decision.

One of my roles is to act as a clinical commissioner for maternity services in North Lancashire. A recent survey of women leaving our maternity service was positive in many ways, but one statistic was cause for alarm: 44 percent felt that they were not treated with kindness or understanding by our staff.[3] In looking at this finding more closely, it transpired that their dissatisfac-

3. S. Wells, *Maternity Picker and Patient Experience Survey*, UHMB NHS Foundation Trust, January 2014.

tion was particularly due to poor communication skills especially around decision-making. Women felt that at key moments in their care, they were not listened to, choices were taken away from them without explanation, and they felt forced into certain aspects of care without understanding why.

Armed with this information, work has begun to look at how communication can be improved so that care is carried out in partnership, with compassion, especially when there are difficult and sometimes life-saving or life-changing decisions to be made. The hope is that it will allow clinicians to hear and understand the needs of women and begin to alter the power dynamics and reconfigure relationships so that women no longer feel disempowered and disrespected.

(iii) Challenging injustice

There are thousands of loving acts carried out daily in every part of our health systems—by people who may be seen as "irritants" to the target-driven culture. However, it is all too easy for those who are loving and kind, who choose not to become hardened, to become burnt out. Systems which allow workers to be so tightly squeezed need to be challenged and changed. Too often I see co-workers, from consultants to cleaners, in need of time off work, primarily as a result of stress.

When I was working across the Medical and Emergency Departments in a hospital in Greater Manchester, the experience was one of chronic understaffing, a crippling number of patients coming through the doors, and bullying by the management. The government target, by which they rate and either reward or penalize Emergency Departments, aims to ensure that 95 percent of people who visit the unit will be seen, treated, and either discharged or admitted within four hours. While this is not altogether bad, and in theory could ensure safer and more immediate care, there were severe repercussions for staff if a patient ever "breached" (went over their allotted four hours). This not only created a culture of distress and fear, but also of lying and, consequently, poor care. Either the record of a patient's time in the department would be altered, and so the real problem would be hidden, or their care would suffer.

After one extremely difficult night when I was covering admissions for the medical unit I wrote to every consultant and manager in the hospital detailing the poor care I had witnessed—and every junior doctor in the hospital signed it. The authorities made a number of threats, including warnings that career prospects would be in jeopardy. Those of us who were training to become GPs and had no intention of hospital careers took the decision to highlight to our college that we felt the training environment was unsafe, bullying, and ineffective. This changed everything, since our college could withdraw its trainees, severely impacting the functioning of the hospital. A full review was carried out and, over a process of about five years, the entire management, including the CEO, was replaced.

PROTEST AND PROCLAMATION

Traditional protest can often seem ineffective. In September 2013 50,000 people marched in Manchester to demonstrate against the current changes being made to the NHS in England[4] – the largest such protest for a generation. It was entirely ignored by the government and the media barely reported it, however.[5] If Jesus was set against systems that operated in unjust and domineering ways, then we have a mandate to challenge existing structures and operate instead out of hope for new ways of being. It is for us to say to unjust and oppressive systems, "be thrown into the sea,"[6] and allow our "prophetic imaginations" to dream new ways of being.

This is particularly important given that the NHS is currently going through one of the biggest top-down reorganizations in sixty-five years, at a cost of more than £2 billion. Despite a

4. http://www.bbc.co.uk/news/uk-england-manchester-24286582.

5. http://labourlist.org/2013/09/burnham-writes-to-bbc-over-lack-of -coverage-for-nhs-march-and-rally.

6. Myers, *"Say to This Mountain"*, *Mark's Story of Discipleship*, 145–52.

government promise that such a reorganization would not happen, more services are being driven out of a traditional hospital setting into the community, with few extra resources or time provided to do this work. Many fear it is the end of the NHS as we have known it and that privatization of care will follow.[7]

The Transatlantic Trade and Investment Partnership, a bilateral EU–US trade agreement, and the General Agreement of Trade of Services (GATS) at the hands of the World Trade Organization (WTO) have opened the NHS, like never before, to the forces of the free-market. Any private healthcare company from a partnership nation can now bid to win any health contract up for tender in the UK. The agreement is based on a philosophy that competition between companies drives up standards of care. At first it may sound plausible to suggest that it benefits the service to choose a provider that can offer the same service for less money. But it is problematic on two levels.

Firstly, this philosophy itself is flawed. In practice, competition very often does not drive up standards.[8] It often increases stress and breaks apart well-integrated services. It destabilizes services which currently work well in a symbiotic manner. This has happened in my local setting where Virgin Healthcare took over the dermatology service, but then found it to be unprofitable and eventually pulled out, leaving the service in a significant mess with long waiting lists and a lack of consultant care.

Secondly, when companies limited by shares become the providers of care, care becomes secondary to the need to make money. And here is a major stumbling block. Caring for the poor and the chronically sick does not make good financial sense, and shareholders who live in another part of the world care little for their needs. If greedy corporations become the providers of "care," those who need healthcare the most will undoubtedly miss out. This is sadly proven in the US health system, where this philosophy is rife: 50 million people cannot afford healthcare and 40,000 people died

7. Pollock and Price, *From Cradle to Grave*, 174–203.

8. L. Reynolds, *Competition and the 1987-2011 NHS Reform*, July 20, 2011, http://www.bmj.com/content/343/bmj.d4136?tab=responses.

last year as they waited for operations they needed but could not afford.[9] While some politicians and sections of the media seem to heavily favor a US-style health system, the majority consider it to be inequitable and highly wasteful of resources.

As a direct result of new policy, driven by the trade agreement, small community practices are now seeking to federate with one another so that they can compete with private providers for the services they already provide.

Most General Practices in this country are run by private partnerships. The basis on which they are run is extremely different to a company limited by shares—though they can absolutely be driven by greed if partners are so motivated. A practice earns money according to the number of patients registered and for providing various services, like vaccinations and smear tests, and through meeting a variety of targets. The money earned then pays the staff in the practice, including the doctors, nurses, other healthcare workers, managers, and administrative teams. If any provider, like Virgin Healthcare, for example, can come in and bid to provide all the vaccinations across the county at a lower cost than these GPs are currently able to provide, it might sound like a good idea from a strictly financial point of view. However, it can also serve to destabilize the practice and removes key services from a local community setting, causing staff to lose their jobs. What this approach also reveals is a government failure to understand the impact caused by taking traditional services out of a local setting, thus breaking some key encounters that doctors and nurses have with patients. A recent report entitled "Saving money by doing the right thing"[10] showed that scaling up local systems into regional ones can be both wasteful and damaging to care.

9. B. Sanders, *Health Care: U.S. vs Canada*, March 12, 2014, https://www.youtube.com/watch?v=iYOf6hXGx6M&feature=youtu.be.

10. J. Seddon, http://locality.org.uk/wp-content/uploads/Locality-Report-Diseconomies-web-version.pdf.

CREATIVE SOLUTIONS

The challenge and great opportunity in General Practice right now is to form federations. In my opinion, these shouldn't be Companies Limited by Shares (CLS), or even Community Interest Companies, despite the fact that these have some ethical strengths compared to the CLS. There is potential for the introduction of cooperative, social-enterprise models, which could draw on the heritage of both the Quaker and Cooperative movement in the North-West. The cooperative model creates the opportunity for a radical overhaul of power, a true sharing of resource and gift, and a letting go of unfair monetary advantages created by our current systems.[11] There is the opportunity for the letting go of unfair monetary advantage by the few so that everybody is able to share the benefit. In forming cooperative federations—and this can apply for all individual practices as well—there is the choice to allow all staff to become shareholders together, not just the doctors. In areas where this happens, such as Surrey Central Healthcare (built on similar principles to the retail business John Lewis Partnership), or the health cooperatives of the Basque region, for example, there is an extremely high sense of morale amongst the staff and high patient satisfaction rates.[12] This reflects a truth that can be uncomfortable for the powerful—that cooperation and not competition drives up both happiness and excellence. There is radical potential also for all members of a local population to become members of a cooperative for health, a model which could expand into education.

St Paul wrote to the Galatians[13] that they were set free for freedom. Jesus told us that we are the light of the world.[14] Revolution doesn't have to be violent and bloody. Revolution can occur

11. Harrison, *People Over Capital, The Co-operative Alternative to Capitalism.*

12. http://www.coownershipsolutions.co.uk/why-co-ownership/what-is-it.

13. Gal 5:1.

14. Matt 5:14.

when enough people choose to engage, to love, and to become the change they want to see. No one system is the answer. Cooperatives will go some way to disarm the powerful, but one only needs to look at the debacle of the Co-operative Bank in the UK to know that it would be foolish, to say the least, to suggest that such a system could solve everything.

Participatory economics could also play an important role if it went beyond isolated budgeting. For example, problems in maternity care and neonatal care are made much more complex by rising rates of obesity and diabetes. Solving the problem requires not only funding aimed at tackling the causes, but collaboration between health and education. Too often they are in competition with one another, however, and while an enormous amount of money is spent on treating disease, or prevention through vaccination programs, nowhere near enough is spent on promoting health in our communities.

One local community cannot provide all of the health needs. Therefore, partnerships between towns and cities could develop in order to both share—and gift—resource to one another. The pharmaceutical industry, advertising giants, the alcohol industry, and fast food chains wield tremendous power in relation to government policy. If health and education budgets were amalgamated and local people involved in deciding how the available resources are distributed, with some basic ground rules to protect the marginalized poor in place, there could be real possibilities for change. The role of leadership in this setting would be to safeguard the priority of care for women, children, the elderly, mentally ill, the marginalized poor, prisoners, and asylum seekers, including the hundreds of people currently held in any one of the eleven detention centers around the UK, having failed in their asylum claim.

TRANSFORMING THE SPHERE

At a community and city level, there are relationships to be deepened and strengthened, and new ways of relating and cooperating to be found. There are "holy experiments" to be done around emptying out power and encouraging the voices of the marginalized to find their place. There are facilitated conversations to be had and new ways of participating in decisions around resources and economics to be discovered. There is new understanding to be forged around how cities can partner together in gift economies.[15]

There is a rising need to comprehend how the local carries a global responsibility. National boundaries and nation states need to be subverted as relational networks develop across the globe and teams begin to find one another to help build healthy communities. Those working across the global setting need to learn how to relate locally to establish justice. Nye Bevan, the founder of the NHS, said this in 1952: "Soon, if we are not prudent, millions of people will be watching each other starve to death through expensive television sets." There is an enormous amount of work to be done across the nations of the earth to see justice established and peace increased.

Transformation requires a realignment and resetting of our priorities. It has become the wisdom of the day to believe that money must drive healthcare. But money is only one resource amongst many—it should be our servant and not our master.

Jesus said something very challenging: "But seek first His kingdom and His righteousness, and all these things will be added to you."[16] Jesus proved that pouring life out in love and emptying power to empower others is the best way for humanity. If we seek the peace and health of our cities and communities, if we pursue goodness over greed and embrace joy over the need to meet targets, then we will find every resource we need will be there in abundance. We hope for the physical, mental, spiritual, emotional, and social wellbeing of everyone, we have faith that healing is everywhere and available for all, and so we know that love holds the key to our hope and our faith as we embrace together a reimagined future.

15. Eisenstein, *Sacred Economics*.
16. Matt 6:33.

7

Seeking the Shalom of the City [1] . . .

Mike Love

TOGETHER FOR PEACE (T4P)[2] began life in 2002 with a vision for a festival that would encourage and support the city of Leeds to respond to the issues of conflict, justice, and peace-making. The context at the time included the aftermath of 9/11, increasing numbers of refugees coming to Leeds, and rising Islamophobia. Following the success of the first one in 2003, further festivals took place in 2005 and 2007 and engaged over 150 different partner organizations and many thousands of people. Since 2005 T4P has carried community development and community relations work at the dividing lines of the city, winning several awards including the national Awards for Bridging Cultures in 2010 and Leeds City Council's Partner Organisation of the Year in 2012.

1. Jer 29:7.
2. t4p.org.uk.

This chapter is an attempt to view our experience and work from a kenarchic perspective.

PEACE?

Early in T4P's life, someone said to us: "Peace is a gift. It isn't something you are responsible for building, creating, bringing into the city; because it is out of your control, all you can do is create spaces where something might happen, where people might discover peace." This peace is outside of, and other than, the "peace" that is created, maintained, and protected by sovereignty and control. Peace is found in the embrace of chaos and of "the other"; both are feared by those who believe "peace" has to be protected by boundaries and barricades. Peace as gift emerges in serendipitous encounters, and is held by human bonds of relationship. Implicit in our understanding of peace is the pursuit of justice and the inevitable conflict with the powers-that-be.

We started out with a question: what would it mean for Leeds to be a "workshop for peace"? This question, encompassing the city as a whole and all its parts, led us to think and work systemically. It gave us permission to experiment, to take risks, and to learn through trial and error.

Wesley Howard-Brook and Anthony Gwyther, in their political reading of the Revelation of St John, *Unveiling Empire*, say, "Empire is depicted as both prostitute and beast—it either seduces you or it destroys you." I find power seductive—I want to be approved of and legitimated by people with power, and I recognize that as a middle-class, educated, white male my natural affinity and my self-interest lie with such people. At the same time I am afraid of the power they have to destroy our work and, even worse, our reputation! I struggle to hold this in tension with a transcendent knowledge that "You would have no power over me if it were not given to you from above."[3] Some of our encounters with sovereignty in the city have been bruising.

3. John 19:11 NIV.

A few days before writing a first draft of this chapter I had meetings with the Leader and Chief Executive of Council to ask for their commitment to a city-wide poverty initiative. I was keenly aware of my interior struggle with these forces. Whether or not I believe this power is real, the fact is I am intimidated by it. Intimidation needs no outer force to keep us compliant with sovereignty.

POWER AND LOVE

Much of our work is about holding space for people to encounter each other across spaces of difference and otherness using dialogue and conversation. We have also used film as "virtual space" to bring people together, with a series of five films under the generic title *In One City*.

There can be no peace without justice, and the larger part of justice is economic justice. In 2008 we were commissioned by Yorkshire Forward, the Regional Development Agency, to make a film[4] exploring people's views on the regeneration of a former industrial area that had been turned into an "urban village" promoting digital technologies. We soon discovered a mismatch between what had been claimed for the economic benefits to the surrounding "rim" communities (typically the poorest neighborhoods with older housing on the rim of the city center) and the actual lived experience of those communities. Knowing the film would cause controversy, extraordinary effort went into the edit until we were satisfied it was a faithful record of all we had heard from residents, developers, and local government officers. The film maker, Dave Tomalin of Lippy Films, was in any case committed to giving everyone he filmed editorial control of their bit of the film and input into the whole. Despite this, senior council officers and some councilors aggressively accused us of slanting the message of the film to undermine the Council's messages about the regeneration project. We knew the finished film was true to what we had heard and that we did not need to defend it, or ourselves.

4. *Ripples Out* by Lippy Films available on YouTube.

In attacking, and then ignoring, the film, they were doing the same to the people whose views did not coincide with theirs. But, being committed to working systemically through relationships and therefore reliant on trust, we really feared we would be cut off from opportunity to work with the Council in the future. Yorkshire Forward (the RDA) stood strongly by us and the film, and vindication came shortly afterwards when the CEO (who loved the film) was appointed Chief Executive of Leeds City Council. He has recently commissioned us to make a similar film about inequalities in the city[5] and the *Ripples Out* film itself continues to travel far and wide and have impact.

Two years later we carried out a listening exercise on one of the poorest estates as the first stage of a "good relations"[6] process for which we had been commissioned by Leeds City Council. Once again, when we reported what we had heard, we found ourselves being strongly criticized by senior council officers who did not like what they heard. They abruptly brought the project to an end and we were blamed for its failure. At the time I was Vice-Chair of the city's Harmonious Communities Partnership Board to which this project was accountable and where I had to face the people who were condemning our work. This was one of the hardest times of my working life as I struggled to deal with feelings of failure, humiliation, and anger towards senior council officers at the same time as having to come to terms with doubtless being seen as yet another short-lived initiative that did nothing to change things for the better on the estate. I had no doubt that we were wrestling with "the powers" in the city that seemed intent on silencing voices that were disruptive of official and political narratives. Some timely reading, John D. Caputo's *The Weakness of God,* helped me to see that to embrace, and not fear, weakness and failure might just be God's way for us to engage the powers.

Both of these projects were about justice and power. We were doing this work because we believed that enabling people to really hear "the other" would increase the possibility of social justice (and

5. *Inequality & Wellbeing: In One City Leeds* available on YouTube.
6. centreforgoodrelations.com.

therefore peace) in the city. We needed to bring people together to do this work and that required their trust in us, and yet we also needed to wrestle with and against oppressive and dominating power. Adam Kahane's *Power and Love* explores Martin Luther King's statement: "Power without love is reckless and abusive, and love without power is sentimental and anaemic. Power at its best is love implementing the demands of justice, and justice at its best is power correcting everything that stands against love." Power can be generative or degenerative—generative when it is "power to . . . " and "power with . . . ," degenerative when it is "power over . . . " Similarly with love: generative when it gives "power to . . .," degenerative when it withholds power. Change will only come when both power and love are in play. Kahane, suggesting generative power and love are dichotomic, likens the dynamic between them to walking—a perpetual imbalance on each leg. As you are taking the power step, you are moving to take the love step, and so on; you can't take both at the same time and you can't stay balanced on just one leg. This has been an important insight for our work generally, and in both these situations taking the power step meant to submit and embrace the little death of failure and shame (as a way of disarming the powers), and not to retreat or renege on our commitment to continue with this kind of work. The love step meant refusing to take an oppositional and antagonistic stance towards the people who opposed us, and in one case inviting the senior council officer whose behavior had angered me most to meet for coffee, when, outside of role and function, we were able to encounter and connect with each other as human beings.

The dominant power defines roles, grants legitimacy, and controls the distribution of resources; and it seeks to co-opt or control anything which may threaten its hegemony. It claims, and is given by citizens, the right to define what is good for the peace of the city and to protect the city from disruptions of that peace. There are inner as well as outer barriers to taking up the mantle to challenge and disrupt it. We are brought up to comply with sovereignty and unconsciously subscribe to its legitimacy and divine right. Much of the voluntary and community sector has become dependent on state funding, and the ability to get large and valuable commissions and contracts is often perceived to be the benchmark of success.

To subvert the powers that keep this "peace" has entailed inner conflict, personally and within our team. What right or light do we have to judge the actions of others? Dare we risk the reputation of T4P when, in order to work systemically across the city, we need people to have faith in us? What do I know, compared with the people whose job it is to know all that needs to be known about how to fight crime, deliver best outcomes in health, or ensure the city is economically prosperous? What difference can my tiny contribution make when set against the huge resources and power of others? Who am I, unelected and without a constituency of any kind (not even a church congregation), to question people who have democratic legitimacy and statutory responsibility, or economic power? Faith fuels the struggle not to be dazzled by and conformed to the legitimating criteria. Maurice Glasman, Labour peer and academic, has said[7] that he sees his own Jewish tradition as both a bulwark against the current hegemony and a resource for struggling with these questions and doubts. The name "Israel" means to struggle, to wage "jihad," and we need to learn to trust our struggle.[8]

We have chosen to be radically independent in order to be able at times to subvert, but at other times to work closely with the powers-that-be in the city. This has been helped by both not having much money for the first few years, and then by having generous independent funding.

From the outset, to stage the 2003 festival we needed to engage diverse organizations, groups, institutions, and communities, each with its own agenda and self-interest and suspicious of ours. We soon realized we were working in a (small p) political world but, because our agenda was not to gain power but to seek the good of the whole through the voluntary sum of its parts, we quickly came to enjoy significant trust from our partners and

7. Speaking at T4P's 2011 "Leeds Summit": www.summat.org.
8. "trust your struggle": poem and photograph by Jez Green, Manchester.

developed our praxis always to work in partnership and never unilaterally. We saw ourselves primarily in a mediative role, brokering relationships across different sectors and communities, and catalyzing collaborations.

It seems that nearly all voluntary organizations want to expand, scale up, and scale across (currently it is all about survival and mergers). We realized that the secret of our success, in this political world, lay in being weak and in remaining as small and organizationally light as we possibly could. T4P has no employees and no property. The core team of three[9] are self-employed and we occupy rent-free premises with no security of tenure. When work has needed more people we have worked with volunteers, with self-employed associates, and with other organizations which can supply our lack. We have consciously chosen to be interdependent. Our team is without hierarchy and we are grateful that our charity trustees fully support our way of working.

We have often been asked if we have plans to expand to other towns and cities but it seems to us that to do so would be to engage in empire building. Each place is particular, and an attempt by us to impose our model would not respect the particularity of place and people. T4P has grown out of and within its particular context and web of relationships.

In contrast to the Politics which is the will to power of a particular faction, (small p) politics is the art of living together, the art of conversation that enables all voices to be heard, the art of peace-building, of love worked out between us.

Jonathan Sacks' book *The Dignity of Difference* has been formative for me, especially his idea that society is a conversation scored (as in music score) for many voices. Leeds, with the most diverse population of any UK city outside London, has the potential (yet to be realized) to facilitate, and be vastly enriched by, this conversation.

We were conscious that if we wanted to connect people and broker relationships across the city, we needed more creative ways of having meetings and enabling conversation. In 2008 I stumbled

9. Jill Mann, Ed Carlisle, and Mike Love.

across the Art of Hosting network[10] through attending a training on "The Art of Hosting Conversations that Matter" and discovered methodologies such as open space, circle, world café, and appreciative inquiry. Through this we have learned ways to bring people together where all voices are listened to and shared wisdom discovered, where purpose is the invisible leader, and leadership itself is redefined as convening and hosting a collaborative space where something might happen. These methodologies actively support the way of love—shared humanity, vulnerability, relationship, trust, co-creation, collaboration—and have in-built immunity to hegemony and domination.

T4P works on the dividing lines of the city. Stanley Hauerwas (quoting Iris Murdoch) says, "love is the non-violent apprehension of the other as Other. But to see the Other as other is frightening because to the extent others are Other they challenge my way of being."[11] Diversity is good and is part of the wonder of creation—the deep sub-soil. Becoming conscious of difference can lead to fear and suspicion. Division is the top soil in which the tree of conflict can grow. Most of the time, little attention is given to the soil and sub-soil, with huge resources concentrated on the fruit of the tree of conflict. Much of T4P's work is preventative, and therefore unquantifiable. It is easier to say why a riot happened and what it cost, than why it didn't happen and what was saved. (Leeds avoided any significant disturbance in the summer of 2011 despite the aggravating factor of a murder across racial lines.)

We actively promote the goodness of diversity through, for example, Planet Leeds, an inter-cultural music festival, and the *In One City* film series. We help people cross dividing lines with programs such as Jewish-Muslim dialogue (including a learning journey together to Israel-Palestine); the Active Citizens project between African-Caribbean and Asian young adults; and the Poverty Truth Challenge, bringing together people with direct personal experience of poverty with civic leaders to work on the city's responses to poverty. We have been inspired by peace-builder

10. www.artofhosting.org.

11. Hauerwas, *The Peaceable Kingdom*, 91.

and academic Jean Paul Lederach, who discovered that effective peace-building after conflict involves weaving strategic relational webs across the community, where the relationships are personal and not merely organizational. We believe that this can also be prophylactic work, strengthening the resilience of the city. Leeds experienced this following the London bombings in 2005 when it was discovered the alleged perpetrators came from Leeds. In the two areas of the city most affected, strong relationships had been formed between Christian and Muslim community leaders, which, in the time of testing, supported both communities to stand together in unity and solidarity.

In the newly super-diverse cities of Europe, the deep human need for community will create exclusionary ghettos if it does not embrace "the other." The new community will be worthy of its name only if it is radically open to "the other." The politics of love that will enable this peaceable community to develop and flourish will have developed the art of this intercultural conversation.

8

Kenarchy and an Eschatological Hope

Martin Scott

ESCHATOLOGY HAS OFTEN BEEN the domain of the marginal, the fantasists, and those with a propensity to seeing the whole world as caught in a web of deception that only some version of conspiracy theory can explain. However, eschatology is more than the foretelling of the future, and an implicit eschatological hope often feeds behavior and response, even among those who do not claim any eschatological framework.

Hope, both theologically and sociologically, is a strong term and one that is inextricably linked to that of "faith." In the context of this chapter "faith" and "worldview" are all-but synonymous. Belief—what I profess I believe—might part company from my expressed worldview, but faith that is enacted seldom does. Faith interprets the world, and the world that is experienced shapes faith. It is this faith, whether Christian or not, that is the fuel for hope.

Inspired, of course by the Scriptures, Christians have a faith-perspective of the world. "The world is the way it is because . . ." and faith fills in the blanks. When pressed further, a description of the future can be forthcoming that then spills over into relevant actions and responses.

TWO DOMINANT ESCHATOLOGIES

Over the past 100 years there are two opposing eschatologies that have influenced the Christian faith. I do not suggest they are the only two but they do continue to fuel expectations and therefore practice. Although variations of them, particularly the second view we will look at, have been around for much longer, it is since the early twentieth century that they have exerted their power.

A dominant eschatological belief that has framed much of evangelical Christianity has its roots in the Dispensationalist movement that sprang from the 1830s. From the late nineteenth century, and with the subsequent publication of the Scofield Bible,[1] this movement influenced generations of evangelicals to lose touch with any real hope of society being shaped for good and diminished motivation to be involved. This view taught that the closing "church-age dispensation" would be expressed with a lukewarm faith, and in the wider world there would be the growth of evil leading to the forces of evil overcoming the world, instituting an inevitable one-world government complete with an antiChrist ruler.

The hope in this context became one of escape. A belief in the "secret rapture" of the true believer that could take place at any time replaced the historic prayer of the church for there to be an appearing of the Lord ("Maranatha"). The final state of things would be the burning up of this world; therefore only eternal things could have any value (and by "eternal" what was really meant was "non-material"). So this approach, presenting as it does a hope for escape, inevitably resulted in no expectation for transformation and a correspondingly all-but absent concern over ecological issues.

---

1. Scofield, *The Old Scofield Study Bible*.

Any commitment to improve society found little encouragement in this movement as the only real task was the work of evangelism that was defined dualistically as "saving souls" so that they too could be ready for the Rapture and escape the Great Tribulation. The line dividing evil and good was very simple and easy to draw. Christian believers were on one side and the world on the other. Thus, feeding straight from ancient Greek dualism there was no thought of stewardship of creation, and the creation mandate to "rule and to multiply," if even thought about, was fulfilled through (ab-)using the world and controlling whatever was necessary.

The second eschatological source has affinity to the classic post-millennial optimistic hope and as such can claim a much longer history within Christian theology. It has been given a major new lease of life through movements such as Reconstructionism and becomes a natural direction that many optimistic charismatic-Pentecostals wish to move toward. These believers can come in many related forms, and in putting them together I am not suggesting that they are all bedfellows, but the pull to this kind of optimistic transformation of the world is something that is held in common. They might have a flavor of being "revival-believing," "transformation-focused," or they might be involved in aggressive "spiritual warfare," or in setting their stall out as seeing the kingdom of heaven manifest through supernatural signs. It is not so much the individual terms or beliefs per se that present the problem, but it is the practice or method that is employed to move toward the goal that is critical.

Although, inevitably, there are great variations as to what is taught, the common strand is of the manifestation to some significant level of the order of heaven within society. In classic post-millennial terms, this was described as an eventual "golden age," the coming of the millennial rule of Christ within history. In these more recent schools of thought, the terms used are more often of a "Victorious Eschatology" where the numerical growth of those finding faith in Christ increases and the influence of Christianity within society grows likewise. Some have also spoken of "sheep" and "goat" nations: where there will be nations that are discipled in the ways of kingdom and nations that will be rebellious against that influence.

KENARCHY AND AN ESCHATOLOGICAL HOPE

On the surface a kenarchic-oriented eschatological hope has more in common with the latter view than the former. This "Victorious Eschatological" view encourages an engagement with this world as is, and the historic kenarchic event of the incarnation has its foundation in that context too. The incarnational pouring out is the bridge between the divine and the human, heaven and earth, the spiritual and the material, and of course the future and the present. There is very little that kenarchists can hold in common with the first dualistic view, as there the hope presented is non-kenarchic, being one of self-preservation.

Yet we have to press these comparisons and contrasts further, for it is not only the expressed hope that is important, but any methodology employed. When an interaction of kenarchy and eschatological hope is explored it soon becomes evident that it is at the point of methodology that there will be a separation from the second outlined view.

In the first century there was significant agreement about hope. The restoration of Israel was a living hope; the belief in the fulfillment of the ancient Jewish covenants was shared in common among the various Jewish sects. How to realize that fulfillment was the ground where the sects parted company, and none envisioned nor were prepared for the kenarchic route.

Likewise, without a kenarchic frame, the proclamation that "Jesus is Lord" can be interpreted as the need to activate believers to become part of the core—perhaps the "top" 3 percent of society that influence the whole. Without a kenarchic understanding we can set out to Christianize the world, to conquer for Jesus, for after all Scripture says that righteousness exalts a nation. The results might not be as extreme as the violent mediaeval Crusades that set out to capture the "holy city" for Jesus, but nevertheless the drive can be to set out a program, implicit or explicit, that eventually proves to have borne no resemblance to the incarnation.

We could state that kenarchy and eschatology need to be intertwined—indeed, they must be held together as eschatology is kenarchic. If we do not grasp this, we can embrace a belief that the goal is to have a Christian at the "top" and a corresponding government that will legislate acceptable morality (sadly normally defined with regard to sexual practice and the protection of the unborn while conveniently avoiding the wider social issues of nationalism and poverty). This falsely founded belief will then, with the inevitable collapse of Christendom in the West, simply fuel a level of disappointment.

There is a further important dimension where kenarchy will shape our eschatological vision. The two views outlined above have something in common in that they have a strong tendency to view the world negatively; it is "evil." One view suggests it will be destroyed and our hope in the immediate is to escape when things get tough and to inhabit heaven in the ultimate future. The other sees the world as in need of total transformation and that being effected through an inherent top-down methodology. Kenarchy is a pouring out into this world, not a withdrawing from it, nor a transformation of it from a height, but a being-submerged-to-the-depths within it, which is expressed in being joined to it.

Let's now place some kenarchic eschatological perspectives into this so that we see how expectation and action can be shaped.

INCARNATION

If our model for kenarchy is the incarnation[2] a key element is to realize that although there was a historic beginning to the incarnation, there is no end to it. Although the incarnation has a historic beginning with "the Word became flesh," in a very real sense it is eternal. The incarnation through to the Ascension forever establishes human representation within the Godhead, but this did

2. Phil 2:5–11.

not bring about a change to the eternal nature of God, but rather clarified the true eternal nature of God. The Lamb slain—perhaps the central imagery of the book of Revelation—was destined to be slaughtered "from the foundation of the world."[3]

The important element for our eschatological hope is the understanding that the incarnation has not ceased nor will it come to an end. The Last Adam continues as the mediator between God and humanity, for he himself is (not was) human.[4] It is the resurrection that makes permanent, so that death is indeed swallowed up, and in the resurrection the Second Person of the Trinity is forever Jesus of Nazareth. The ultimate hope of the Parousia might be couched in imperial language but is so only to subvert all imperial expectation. The disciples were told that, "This Jesus, who has been taken up from you into heaven, will come in the same way as you saw him go into heaven."[5] The profundity of those words are not to be lost in the futile discussion of direction of up/down, and certainly not with regard to the timing of this event. There is a profound continuity between the Jesus of history and the One who will come. The Jesus who returns will be the same Jesus who has taken up temporary residence in "heaven." We do not wait for another Jesus, but for the *same* Incarnate Jesus. The Jesus who comes again will not advocate another pathway, so that the Sermon on the Mount turns out to be simply temporary advice until full and normal control can be restored, and by restored what is really meant is "imposed." To suggest otherwise is to subvert the eternally motivated act of incarnation.

LANGUAGE

Language is a God-given tool that is intrinsic to our humanity. In God there is communication—the biblical Hebrew writer does not waste breath to argue over the existence of God, for we read that

3. Rev 13:8; Acts 2:23; 1 Pet 1:19–20.

4. 1 Tim 2:5.

5. Acts 1:11.

"In the beginning . . . God spoke." In God speech is not simply a set of words, or concepts, as there is no gap between what he says and who he is. His words are life-giving.

Too often words are captivated to enforce a dominant viewpoint. This was the way with the imperial worlds of the New Testament era. "Peace" was enforced through war, prosperity through slavery and hierarchy. I observe that not too much has changed there.

The language of the New Testament is undoubtedly intensely political; hence the accurate understanding that Paul was indeed proclaiming another king.[6] The gospel of peace was an explicit critique of the "Pax Romana," the kingdom (*basileia*) of God was a direct exposure of the Roman empire (*basileia*), and the insistence that "Jesus is Lord" instantly defined that Caesar, in spite of his claims as a son of god, was not lord.

Kenarchy is a lens that helps us interpret language, for there is militant language that surrounds some of the eschatological passages of Scripture. However, New Testament language is not replacing like with like. We are not to think that if we take the kingdom of Rome, clean it up some, we then have a picture of the kingdom of heaven. We do not model what is "there" and will be "then" on what is "here" and "now." I can illustrate this in the Old Testament movement from:

- God is king
- Israel rejects God as king, wanting to be as the other nations, and asks for a human king
- There are good and bad kings
- We then (wrongly) assume that the good kings are a model of God as king. And that we can define sovereignty as a good version of human kingship.

Sovereignty is not defined through "good" sovereigns. They can be an example of a good version of a bad model, but *the model is still wrong*, it cannot be cleansed.

6. Acts 17:7.

So Jesus is not instituting another version, albeit a good version, of the imperial power of the day and he is not returning to establish it. The idea that his followers were to take up the sword[7] has to be rejected, and likewise we must reject the idea that this same Jesus will one day return with the sword to slay his enemies. That might be the hope that some readers of Scripture carry, but cannot be for those who see through the kenarchic lens.

THE CENTRAL IMAGERY IS OF THE LAMB SLAIN

If Revelation is an unveiling so that we see things clearly, then in four key movements in the book (the four times John marks that he was "in the Spirit") we see four very stark realities that are unveiled: the risen, human, exalted Jesus;[8] the throne room of heaven which all earthly throne rooms parody;[9] the oppressing, dominating, adulterating, exploiting systems that conspire together to feed the center and enslave the margins;[10] and the society of people with the life of God in their midst.[11] Those four movements shape eschatological hope, and the foundation for the glorious final hope lies within the core of the unveiling of the throne room of heaven. Let me first, with the help of Henry Drummond (1851–1897) and his insightfully radical book *The City without a Church*,[12] look at that final (eschatological) vision of the New Jerusalem.

> Two very startling things arrest us in John's vision of the future. The first is that the thing most like heaven he could think of was a city; the second, that there was no church in that city. Almost nothing more revolutionary could be said, even to the modern world, in the name of religion. No church—that is the defiance of religion; a city—that

7. John 18:36.

8. Rev 1:10.

9. Rev 4:2.

10. Rev 17:3.

11. Rev 21:10.

12 Drummond, *The City without a Church*.

> is the antipodes of heaven. Yet John combines these contradictions in one daring image, and holds up to the world the picture of a city without a church as his ideal of the heavenly life.[13]

The vision is not of a creation being destroyed, nor of a people who escape, nor even of a God who has to make new things, but rather One who makes all things new.[14] In that process all temporary dualities come to an end and we conclude that the New Jerusalem is a multivalent image for the fulfillment of eschatological hope. In this new creation vision we see a bride ready to enter marriage so that the two might become one, we discover a people who have followed the Lamb wherever he has gone, and we marvel at the very inner part of the Temple (the cube-shaped Holy of Holies) now no longer being contained in a location, but rather transforming all locations. This New Jerusalem fills the whole of creation, and simultaneously God and the Lamb fill the whole of that city. The movement is synchronous, that is the beauty of it. God's kenarchic love permeating through the followers of the Lamb enables them to pour themselves into the whole of creation, and the pouring out into creation connects with the outpoured presence of God and the Lamb.

This is a radical vision. This future certainly does not rise up from the earth as a testimony to our good deeds for it comes down from heaven. Yet it does not come to us in an other-worldly form. It comes as a fulfilled Temple vision, built by God yet utilizing all the materials of value that the co-workers with God have crafted.[15]

What then is the process that unlocks the movement from creation to new creation? Undoubtedly, in the imagery of the book of Revelation, it is found in the unveiling of the One found worthy to open the scroll. In familiar language John hears that the Lion of the tribe of Judah has overcome and that he can open the book. Familiar language that can be misunderstood. The next experience

13. http://henrydrummond.wwwhubs.com/city.htm Accessed March 17, 2014.

14. Rev 21:5.

15. 1 Cor 3:10–17.

that John records is that after hearing he *sees*. As is so often the case in the book, the sight interprets what has just been heard, and having heard the familiar language he turns to see what is so unfamiliar within the kingdoms of this world. He sees a slain Lamb.

Kenarchy and eschatology are permanently joined. Only the followers of the Lamb (who are not described as followers of the Lion) who follow wherever he goes can also overcome.[16] They have a hope birthed in the kenarchic example of the Lamb. The hope is not for them alone: it is a hope for the re-birth of creation, of the bringing back to purpose of what has been de-railed. And they carry the conviction that the Lamb slain will continue to ride out against all injustice, clothed inevitably in a robe dipped in his own blood. The marks of his own kenarchic death continue.[17]

What a hope then for the future. A society that has no religious center, indeed has no center to it. A place where the pure kenarchic flow of God's life will be throughout it. Future hope is what shapes all action in the here and now.

HOW THEN DO WE RESPOND?

Kenarchy is within the heart of God from all eternity. It is his eternal nature, and the historic Christ event signifies that this marks everything he does and will do. It must also mark the work of those who follow him. Eschatology raises our hope that this same Jesus will return and that there is a relentlessness to his pursuit of the new creation. We then learn how to live in the in-between, the space between the "now" and the "then," with at times the inevitable compromises that are thrust upon us, but the knowledge that there is always a redemptive flow that can be discovered. Even when we feel overwhelmed and trapped and painfully realize that we cannot do what is perfect—and that idea of perfectionism owes more to Greek dualism than to Hebrew holiness—we can indeed engage redemptively. A redemptive response (perhaps we could

16. Rev 14:4.
17. Rev 19:13.

call it a "healing" response) begins as we seek to discern how best to lift what is a fallen manifestation to a still-inadequate but considerably-better-reflection of how things are in heaven.

Eschatology calls for action, it calls for healing, for redemption; it does not inhabit the world of unrealizable idealism.

A kenarchic eschatological hope does not paralyze or strengthen the desire for escape. It defies the pull of self-preservation, and is intensely practical. "Something can be done now" is the response, not "it will be all resolved in the sweet bye and bye." This kind of eschatological hope will look at the challenge within the timeframe of a generation. The eternal kenarchic movement is present within every generation and those who follow the Lamb will proclaim that their "God is able to..." and they will fill in the blank with substance as they know that God's activity is not abstract and conceptual but concrete and historically evident.

Having engaged, albeit, imperfectly we can rest back knowing that what is sown will produce a harvest. After all the activity, the hope that inspired the activity will remain, the hope for transformation, the hope for a city that lives by the light of God. We work, knowing that we are crafting building material for that city. Only he can build it but he will ensure that what has been done in harmony with the foundation of Christ will be the very elements that will form the city.

It is this hope that can be expressed in any and all realms of human life and relationship. It does not matter if it is within the power world of economics or politics or the mercy-realm of the care-professions: a kenarchic-shaped eschatology will help us look at the hope of how things will be and grasp that there has to be a flow of life away from any center to the margins. The goal will not be to impose an agenda but will live with a willingness to be submerged within the systems of this world knowing that those who go to the depth follow the One who will come again. This is far removed from the escapist- and from the dominion-orientated eschatologies that have shaped the mindsets of those within the Christian faith.

Bibliography

Agamben, Giorgio. *State of Exception*. Translated by Kevin Attell. Chicago and London: The University of Chicago Press, 2005.

Ahmed, Leila. *A Quiet Revolution: The Veil's Resurgence, from the Middle East to America*. New Haven: Yale UP, 2011.

Alison. J. *The Joy of Being Wrong: Original Sin Through Easter Eyes*. US: Crossroad Publishing Co., 1998.

Arendt, Hannah. *The Human Condition*. Chicago: University of Chicago Press, 1998.

Badiou, Alain. *In Praise of Love*. Translated by Nicolas Truong. London: Serpent's Tail, 2012.

Balibar, Etienne. "Possessive Individualism reversed: from Locke to Derrida." *Constellations* 9 (2000) 302.

Batson, C. D., N. Ahmad and D. A. Lishner, "Empathy and Altruism." In *The Oxford Handbook of Positive Psychology*, edited by S. J. Lopez and C. R. Snyder, 422. New York: Oxford University Press, 2009.

Boyd, Gregory A. "The Christus Victor View." In *The Nature of the Atonement: Four Views*, edited by James Beilby and Paul R. Eddy, 23-49. Downers Grove, Illinois: IVP Academic, 2006.

Bretherton, Luke. "Love Your Enemies": Usury, Citizenship and the Friend-Enemy Distinction. *Modern Theology* 27 (2011) 369.

Brewin, Kester. *Other: Loving Self, God and Neighbour in a World of Fractures*. London: Hodder & Stoughton, 2010.

Burton, Antoinette M. *Burdens of History: British Feminists, Indian Women, and Imperial Culture, 1865-1915*. Chapel Hill: University of North Carolina, 1994.

Caputo, John D. *The Weakness of God: A Theology of the Event*. Bloomington: Indiana University Press, 2006.

———. *What Would Jesus Deconstruct? The Good News of Post-modernism for the Church*. Grand Rapids, MI: Baker Academic, 2007.

Bibliography

Cavanaugh, William T. *Theopolitical Imagination*. London and New York: T. & T. Clark, 2002.

Critchley, Simon. *The Faith of the Faithless: Experiments in Political Theology*. London and New York: Verso, 2012.

Derrida, Jacques. *Given Time: I. Counterfeit Money*. Translated by Peggy Kamuf. Chicago and London: University of Chicago Press, 1992.

Eisenstein, C. *Sacred Economics*. Berkeley, California: North Atlantic Books, 2011.

Eusebius. *The History of the Church*. Translated by G. A. Williamson. London: Penguin Books, 1965.

Faludi, Susan. *The Terror Dream: Fear and Fantasy in Post 9/11 America*. London: Atlantic, 2008.

Federici, Silvia. *Caliban and the Witch: Women, the Body and Primitive Accumulation*. New York: Autonomedia, 2003.

Fletcher, Paul. *Disciplining the Divine*. Farnham, Surrey and Burlington, Vermont: Ashgate, 2009.

Foucault, Michel. *The History of Sexuality,* vol. I. Translated by Robert Hurley. London: Penguin Books, 1990.

Frankl, Victor E. *Man's Search for Ultimate Meaning*. Kindle edition, 2011.

Fraser, Nancy. *The Fortunes of Feminism: From Women's Liberation to Identity Politics to Anti-Capitalism*. London: Verso Books, 2013.

Girard, René. *Sacrifice*. East Lansing: Michigan State University Press, 2011.

Harding, Sandra. *Whose Science? Whose Knowledge?* New York: Cornell University Press, 1991.

Hardt, Michael, and Antonio Negri. *Multitude*. New York: Penguin Books, 2004.

Harrison, R., ed. *People Over Capital, The Co-operative Alternative to Capitalism*. Oxford: New Internationalist Publications Ltd, 2013.

Hartstock, Nancy. *The Feminist Standpoint Revisited and Other Essays*. Boulder: Westview Press, 1998.

Hauerwas, Stanley. *The Peaceable Kingdom: A Primer in Christian Ethics*. Notre Dame, In.: University Notre Dame Press, 1986.

Hillyard, P. and S. Tombs. "From 'Crime' to Social Harm." In *Crime, Law and Social Change* 48 (2007) 9-25.

Hobbes, Thomas. *Leviathan*. Edited by Richard Tuck. Cambridge: Cambridge University Press, 1996.

Horsley, Richard. *Jesus and Empire*. Minneapolis: Fortress Press, 2003.

Howard-Brook, Wes, and Anthony Gwyther. *Unveiling Empire: Reading Revelation Then and Now*. Maryknoll, New York: Orbis Books, 1999.

Hyde, Lewis. *The Gift: How the Creative Spirit Transforms the World*. Edinburgh: Canongate Books, 2006.

Jersak, Bradley. "We Are Not Our Own. The Platonic Christianity of George P. Grant: From the Cave to the Cross and Back with Simone Weil." PhD diss., Bangor University, 2012.

Kahane, Adam. *Power and Love: A Theory and Practice of Social Change*. San Francisco: Berrett-Koehler Publishers, 2009.

Kearney, Richard. "The Hermeneutics of the Gift: A Dialogue." In *Gift and Economy: Ethics, Hospitality and the Market*, edited by Eric R. Stevenson, 79. Newcastle: Cambridge Scholars Publishing, 2012.

Koltko-Rivera, M. E. "Rediscovering the Later Version of Maslow's Hierarchy of Needs: Self-Transcendence and Opportunities for Theory, Research and Unification." *Review of General Psychology* 10 (2006) 302-17.

Levinas, E., and R. Kearney. "Dialogue with Emmanuel Levinas." In *Face to Face with Levinas*, edited by R. A. Cohen, 13-33. Albany: State University of New York Press, 1986.

Lewis, C. S. *The Lion, the Witch and the Wardrobe*. London: HarperCollins, 2009.

Locke, John. "Second Discourse." In *Two Treatises of Government*. 2nd ed. Edited by Peter Laslett, 285-446. Cambridge & New York: Cambridge University Press, 1988.

Marx, Karl, and Frederick Engels. *The Communist Manifesto: A Modern Edition*. London & New York: Verso, 1998.

McSwain, Jeff. *Movements of Grace: The Dynamic Christo-Realism of Barth, Bonhoeffer, and the Torrances*. Eugene, Oregon: Wipf and Stock, 2010.

Mitchell, Roger Haydon. *Church, Gospel, and Empire: How the Politics of Sovereignty Impregnated the West*. Eugene, Oregon: Wipf and Stock, 2011.

———. *The Fall of the Church*. Eugene, Oregon: Wipf and Stock, 2013.

Murray Williams, Stuart. *Post-Christendom: Church and Mission in a Strange New World (After Christendom)*. Paternoster Press, 2004.

Myers, C. *"Say to This Mountain", Mark's Story of Discipleship*. Maryknoll, New York: Orbis Books, 1996.

Payne, B., V. Conway, C. Bell, A. Falk, H. Flynn, C. McNeil, F. Rice. *Restorative Practices in Northern Ireland: A Mapping Exercise*. Belfast: Queen's University Belfast School of Law, 2010.

Pollock, A., and D. Price. *From Cradle to Grave*. In *NHS SOS*, edited by J. Davis. London: Oneworld Publications, 2013.

Power, Nina. *One-dimensional Woman*. Winchester, UK and Washington, USA: Zero Books, 2009.

Quinlan, C. *Inside: Ireland's Women's Prisons Past and Present*. Irish Academic Press Ltd, 2010.

Rohr, Richard. "The Franciscan Opinion." In *Stricken By God?* Edited by Brad Jersak and Michael Hardin, 208-212. Grand Rapids, Michigan and Cambridge, UK: William B. Eerdmans Publishing Company, 2007.

———. *Falling Upward: A spirituality for the two halves of life*. London: SPCK 2012.

Rousseau, J. "Discourse on Political Economy (first version of the Social Contract)." In *The Social Contract and Other Later Political Writings*, edited by Victor Gourevitch, 23. Cambridge & New York: Cambridge University Press, 1987.

Bibliography

Rowbotham, Sheila. *Hidden from History; 300 Years of Women's Oppression and the Fight against It.* London: Pluto, 1973.

Sacks, Jonathan. *The Dignity of Difference: How to Avoid the Clash of Civilizations.* London: Continuum, 2002.

Schmitt, Carl. *Theory of the Partisan: Intermediate Commentary on the Concept of the Political.* New York: Telos Press Publishing, 2007.

——. *The Concept of the Political.* Chicago and London: University of Chicago Press, 2008.

Scofield, Cyrus I. *The Old Scofield Study Bible,* rev. edn. Oxford University Press, 1909.

Torrance, Thomas. *Incarnation.* Downers Grove, Illinois: InterVarsity Press, 2008.

Tyler, Imogen. *Revolting Subjects: Social Abjection and Resistance in Neoliberal Britain.* N.p.: Zed, 2013.

Virno, Paolo. *The Grammar of the Multitude.* Cambridge, Massachusetts and London, England: MIT Press, 2004.

Volf, Miroslav. "Forgiveness, Reconciliation and Justice." In *Stricken By God?* Edited by Brad Jersak and Michael Hardin, 268-286. Grand Rapids, Michigan and Cambridge UK: William B. Eerdmans Publishing Company, 2007.

Ward, Graham. *Christ and Culture.* Oxford: Blackwell Publishing, 2005.

Weil, Simone. *Gravity and Grace.* Abingdon: Routledge, 2002.